# Simply
# Tassels

## The
## Creative
## Art of
## Design

From the Collection of Nancy Welch

From the Collection of Nancy Welch

From the Collection of Nancy Welch

From the Collection of Nancy Welch

# Simply
# TASSELS
## The Creative Art of Design

Created by Lucia Antonelli

## Nancy Welch

Sterling Publishing Co., Inc.  New York

A Sterling / Chapelle Book

Chapelle:
- Jo Packham, Owner
- Cathy Sexton, Editor
- Staff: Marie Barber, Ann Bear, Areta Bingham, Kass Burchett, Rebecca Christensen, Holly Fuller, Marilyn Goff, Holly Hollingsworth, Shawn Hsu, Susan Jorgensen, Pauline Locke, Barbara Milburn, Linda Orton, Karmen Quinney, Leslie Ridenour, and Cindy Stoeckl

Illustrations/Diagrams:
- Gail Gandolfi

Photography:
- Kevin Dilley, Photographer for Hazen Photography
- Kass Burchett, Photo Stylist for Chapelle

End Papers:

*In this illustration, tassels adorn an award-winning costume designed by Edward Dyas. It has been decorated with more than five hundred tassels.*

If you have any questions or comments, please contact Chapelle, Ltd., Inc., P.O. Box 9252, Ogden, UT 84409 • (801) 621-2777 • (801) 621-2788 Fax • e-mail: Chapelle1@aol.com

A Sterling/Chapelle Book

10 9 8 7 6 5 4 3 2 1

A paperback edition published in 2002 by
Sterling Publishing Company, Inc.
387 Park Avenue South, New York, N.Y. 10016
Originally published in hardcover by Sterling Publishing Co., Inc.
under the title *The Creative Art of Tassels*
© 1999 by Chapelle Ltd.
Distributed in Canada by Sterling Publishing
*c/o* Canadian Manda Group, One Atlantic Avenue, Suite 105
Toronto, Ontario, Canada M6K 3E7
Distributed in Great Britain and Europe by Cassell PLC
Wellington House, 125 Strand, London WC2R 0BB, England
Distributed in Australia by Capricorn Link (Australia) Pty. Ltd.
P.O. Box 704, Windsor, NSW 2756 Australia

*Printed and Bound in China*
*All Rights Reserved*

Sterling ISBN 0-8069-7715-9

From the Collection of Nancy Welch

# Contents

# INTROD

From the Collection of Nancy Welch

In 1977, while I was teaching a fiber arts class, I assigned tassel-making as a project. Little did I realize the extent of homework I had made for myself. After extensive research, I authored a small book on the subject of tassel-making, and in 1991, I authored a second book, *Tassels: The Fanciful Embellishment.*

This book begins where the other two end. It is filled with new and exciting ideas and information for the tassel-making enthusiast, as well as for those who are intrigued by the artistry that goes into the creation of a tassel. Included in these pages is an overview of how to make a simple tassel, including a few fancy knots and cords, but the emphasis is placed on techniques that can be used to personalize your tassels.

Tassel-making isn't a new craft. In fact, people throughout the ages have been making tassels, mostly for their own enjoyment.

# UCTION

Visit a castle in Europe, a Ger in the Gobi, watch *Gone with the Wind* or *Raiders of the Lost Ark,* and you will find a flurry of tassels. They are rooted in both past and present and often serve as a cultural signature.

None of these tassels have a practical purpose, except perhaps to perform the most important function of all: adding sparkle, delight, movement, and visual pleasure to our lives.

I have been fortunate to have people share their knowledge and creation of tassels with me, and many of them have their work displayed in this book.

Outside the Victoria and Albert Museum in London are these words: "The excellence of every art must consist in the complete accomplishment of its purpose."

Tassels are an art form whose only purpose is to provide pleasure and they do this with complete accomplishment.

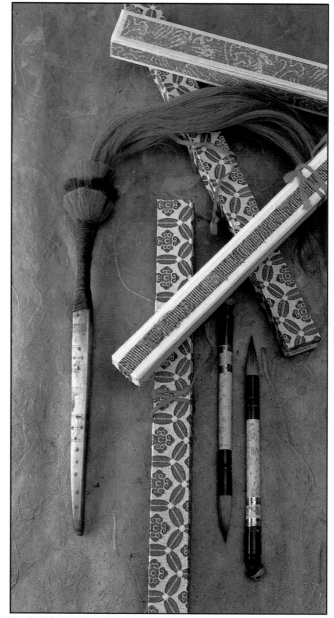

From the Collection of Nancy Welch

*In Niger, nomadic herdsmen adorn themselves with tassels and face paint to attract young women.*

8

# TASSEL
## ELEMENTS & TECHNIQUES

### EVERYTHING STARTS SOMEWHERE

In the case of the tassel, nature is the creator. Archaeologists have discovered corn pollen that is at least 80,000 years old. Without a tassel there would be no pollen!

If the definition of textile is the manipulation of fiber, then tassels could logically be called one of the first textiles. Long before the time of stone, bronze, and iron came the age of vines and grasses.

The first technical skills of humans involved the use of vegetation. The twisting and plaiting of plants allowed the individual some control over his surroundings. The ability to bind and lash provided a means to drag, catch, and carry. Securing the ends of these ropes to prevent raveling gave birth to the tassel.

Examples of twisted fiber used in clothing show up as early as 20,000 years B.C., so it is safe to assume that a simple rope twisted from materials at hand and bound at the ends would predate this sophisticated discovery by millennia. This practical solution to a problem produced a decorative element that has remained throughout the centuries in all cultures and has been reproduced in every conceivable material. Thus, while searching for the beginning, we find the perfect ending.

From the Collection of Nancy Welch

What comes to your mind when you think of a tassel? Formal drapery tiebacks in an elegant home, or folk trappings on a nomad's camel? A graduation tassel hanging from a convertible mirror, or a crocheted tassel in a musty Victorian window? Most tassels are created by individuals simply for their own enjoyment. Almost all are made by hand; others are commercially constructed and mass produced.

Tassels soon outgrew their original practical function and became entities in themselves. Tassels as decorative elements have been in use since at least 3200 B.C.

Before recorded Egyptian history, the tablet of Nar-Mar shows that a cord, worn around the waist with a tassel in front, served as a form of clothing.

The earliest surviving tassel was discovered in the Alps in 1991 on a Stone Age man buried for 5,300 years. His tassel was made of string and attached to a polished stone, not a part of a bound off cord.

**Illustrations in this book show some of the ways tassels have been created. The illustration above is of a Stone Age tassel. The existence of tassels throughout history can be traced in art books, museums, and archeological sites. Tassels turn up in all corners of the world and the variety is astonishing — everything from weapons to women is adorned. Tassels are used by priests, peasants, royalty, and commoners. They play a role in many spiritual and religious functions by shamans, medicine men, Shinto, Christians, Jews, Buddhists, Muslims, and others.**

## GATHER MATERIALS WHERE YE MAY

The procedure for making tassels couldn't be more simple. It is how you put them together that counts. So many fibers are available in such gorgeous colors, that choosing among them may be the most difficult part.

Fibers that can be used include anything from threads to yarns, both natural and synthetic, and you don't need much — it's not like you're going to knit a sweater or weave an afghan.

Nothing is more defeating than a long list of supplies when you are anxious to start a new project. One of the nice things about making tassels is that you need very little; in fact, you may not need to buy anything to get started. Gather up whatever you have around and give it a try!

With the emphasis on and importance of recycling everything these days, take a look around your home and do your part for ecology. Anything that will hang and drape nicely is fair game when creating a tassel.

I have seen tassels made from plastic grocery bags that have been stacked and the handles wrapped to form a top. The bottoms of the bags were clipped to form fringe and then wrapped for the neck. This is the perfect choice if you need a waterproof tassel.

Painted leaves strung on metallic cord, silkworm cocoons formed into a tassel from Thailand, plastic bread-wrapper tassels from Samoa, and an old light bulb adorned with leather fringe made in Timbuktu are just a few of my favorites.

My motto is: "Don't overlook anything when you are thinking tassels!"

Created by Rita Zerull

Created by Sharron Carlton

Created by Doris Hoover

## DYEING TO PLEASE

If the colors of your fibers don't please you, or you feel the finished tassel needs a boost, try a quick dip in the dye pot. Any all-purpose dye, readily accessible at any grocery store, will blend discordant colors, and can be used before or after the tassel is constructed.

To give a cohesive shading, or to produce highlights over the base color, dip the strands or the tassel in a pot of dye. An overdye is often all that is needed to transform an ordinary tassel into an extraordinary one.

To shade the skirt, suspend the tips of the tassel in the dye and let it seep color up. Use a weak solution for soft shadings. If the tassel fibers are wet first, the dye will penetrate more quickly and render a lighter color.

To create a multicolored effect, fold the tassel fibers in half and lay them on a sheet of plastic. Dribble spots of different colors on the strands. Let the fibers sit to absorb the dye. Blot the fibers and hang to dry.

**Each fiber contributes a quality. Silk and rayon have a luscious sheen, metallics add sparkle, wool wears well, while synthetics and blends offer endless color and texture possibilities. You will have no trouble customizing your tassels to any decor. Think tint, texture, sheen, and shine. Tassels are delightful bundles of texture and color. To check how fibers will combine in a tassel, hold up a few strands of each, twist them together at the top, and let the ends dangle. If one of the threads sticks out or the color is wrong, you can easily replace it without having to rewind an entire tassel.**

Created by Jett Thorson

## THE BASIC TASSEL

Tassels are composed of wound fibers divided into four parts: hanger, head, neck, and skirt. The hanger is made from strands referred to as the "cord" and the head, neck, and skirt are the components that make up the "body."

Read through the directions for winding a body for your tassel, choose one of the options for making a cord, and then select a method for connecting them. Additional and diverse design ideas and variations are suggested throughout this book.

The directions are strictly "state-of-the-heart," so no one else will have a tassel quite like yours. If you want a tassel that looks exactly like someone else's, you can buy a commercial one.

## WINDING A BODY AND OTHER ALTERNATIVES

Collect your tassel yarns or alternative fibers, a pair of scissors, and a form. The form should be slightly longer than you want your tassel to be and must be firm, such as a book or heavy piece of cardboard.

## *Try This!*

■ For a finer appearance, untwist plied yarns after the tassel is complete.

■ Mix colors, yarns, and textures. If you are making several tassels in the same color scheme, wind all the threads together on a ball winder first and then wind the tassels from the ball.

**Referring to the diagram above:**

**1. When winding a body for your tassel, first determine the size you want your tassel to be and then choose a form. When making a small tassel, two fingers can be used as the form. Your hand can be used for a larger tassel, and your entire arm and elbow can be used for a long tassel.**

**2. Wind your choice of fiber around the form as many times as you wish.**

**3. Cut across all the fibers at one end and lay them out smoothly in front of you.**

■ To make a "precious" yarn go farther, wind "filler" yarns over the form and then cover them with the special one. The gorgeous yarn becomes the outer layer, but all the yarns will show, so the colors and textures must match.

■ Wind a group of one color next to a group of another color and combine them for a striped tassel. Add an international flavor by using the colors in flags and wrapping with a third color. Red and white tassels with blue wrapping work for France, Great Britain, Iceland, and The Netherlands. Add some gold French knots around the neck of the tassel representing the United States. See illustration below.

■ Wind one color directly over another color, make the tassel, then trim away the top color on one side to reveal the color underneath. Layer colors to create an entire rainbow. See illustration below.

■ To retain the loops at the bottom, rather than cutting the strands, put the form you intend to wind over into a plastic bag, or place a paper sleeve around it. Wind the fibers, then slide it off the form. The strands will be in tact without having to stretch them to get them off the form.

■ To speed things up, don't bother winding. Fold a purchased skein of embroidery floss in half and wrap the neck. See diagrams below.

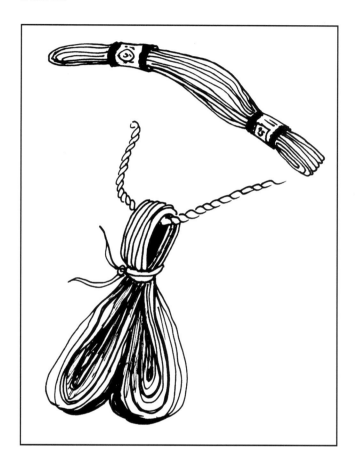

■ Tiny tassels can be sliced with a razor from a spool of thread. See diagram below.

## USING COMMERCIAL TRIMMINGS

Commercial trimmings, such as drapery and upholstery fringe, provide a quick and easy source of tassel-making material without having to wind. There are three basic types of commercial fringe.

*Dipped in a weak dye, this rayon fringe tassel glows with subtle shading.*

Rayon chainette is the easiest to find and comes in many lengths. It is like crochet — if you pull on one end, the chain will unwind and you will have a kinky, curly material twice as long as you started with.

There is also a twisted rayon fringe that unravels on the ends with wear. This type of fringe takes dye nicely and is commonly used as trimming on Victorian lamps. Warning: This type of fringe is very alluring, so tassels made from it may receive a lot of fondling!

The third type of commercial fringe is bullion. The ends are twisted, looped, and plied back on themselves. It is heavier and comes in both plain and mixed colors. It can generally be found in upholstery departments.

Fringes come in several materials: polyester does not drape well; silk is marvelous, but hard to find; and rayon is the most prevalent. If the fringe feels wonderful on the bolt, and the price fits into your budget, then give it a try!

### *Try This!*

  Roll two different lengths and colors of fringe together so one hangs below the other.

■  Wind the bound edge of the fringe into a cone shape to form a beehive or domed top. Include a cord before winding.

**Referring to the diagrams above:**

**1. When using commercial fringe for your tassel, roll the fringe along the bound edge and, if you wish, include a cord as shown in the diagram on the top.**

**2. Or, flip the fringe and wrap a neck below the bound edge. The cord would be laid in the opposite direction as shown in the diagram on the bottom.**

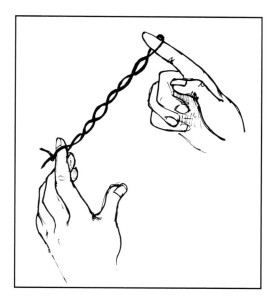

## MAKING A CORD OR ROPE

An elegant tassel deserves an elegant cord. Often-times, a plump tassel dangles limply from a single strand of yarn. Smooth, shiny threads make a crisp cord, textured fibers add interest, but fuzzy yarns tend to obliterate the nice twists.

Referring to
the diagram above:

1. When making a cord for your tassel, measure the yarn approximately five times the desired length of the finished cord.

2. Fold the yarn in half and knot the ends together to form a loop.

3. Hold the knotted end of the loop over one of your index fingers and the other end over your other index finger and start twisting.

4. When the yarn begins to kink, fold the cord in half and let it twist back on itself.

5. Smooth out the twists and tie another knot over the first one to secure both ends of the cord, preventing it from unwinding.

### Try This!

- To add texture and color to your tassel, twist several strands together as one.

- Folding firm yarn in thirds creates a different texture; knot both ends before twisting.

- Three or more thin cords twisted together and doubled back on themselves make a more complex looking rope.

- To place keys or charms on a tassel, slip them onto the twisted cord before you bring the two ends together. See illustration below.

- Make a thin cord by twisting a single piece of thread. Hold on to each end and twist with your fingers — take care, as it will try to get away from you. When it is tightly twisted, bring your fingers together, smoothing the cord and knotting the ends.

- Swag lengths of twisted cord over the tassel skirt for decoration.

- Add ribbons or fabric to the cord either before or after twisting. See diagrams below.

- Make a two-colored cord by looping two lengths together in the middle before twisting. When you bring the ends together, make certain to fold them at the junction of the two colors. See diagram below.

■ Twist lengths of commercial satin piping together to create an elegant cord. Mix two yarn cords with a satin one for another effect. Examine commercial cords for design ideas.

■ Add short lengths of twisted cord to the outside of a tassel skirt for decoration. See illustration below.

■ Slip charms, beads, small covered molds, tiny tassels, or pompons on the cord for added embellishment. See illustrations above.

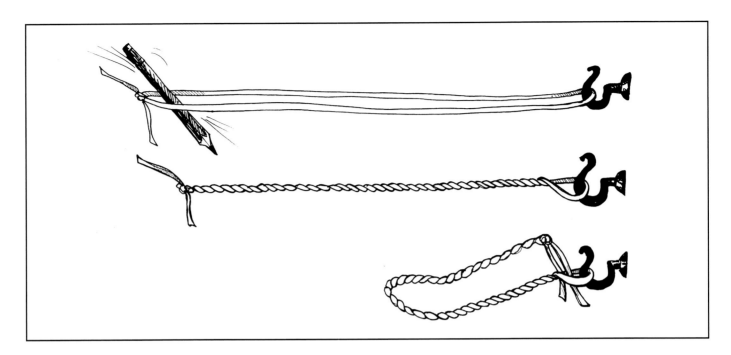

■ For a longer cord than can be achieved with your arm, secure the knotted end over a hook, slip a pencil into the loop, and twist. See diagrams above.

■ For speed in twisting, use a dremel, an eggbeater, or an electric or hand drill attached to one end of the loop with the other end secured. See diagram below.

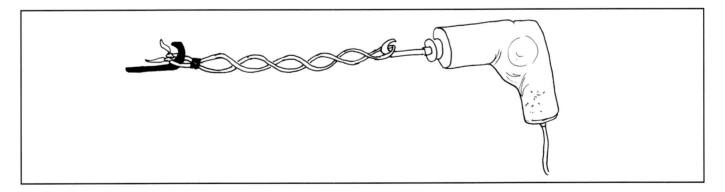

■ When twisting lightweight threads, the bobbin winder on a sewing machine will do the same thing. Any number of threads can be twisted together as one. Attach one end of the threads to the hole in the bobbin and the other end to a pencil. This can be done with the threads in a loop or in one length. Set the machine to wind a bobbin and whirl away, hanging onto the pencil so the line is taut. Two people can make a longer cord: one holding the pencil; the other running the machine.

## MAKING A CORD WITHOUT DOUBLING

When two or more groups of fibers are twisted tightly in one direction and then brought together and twisted in the opposite direction, they will form a cord without having to be doubled.

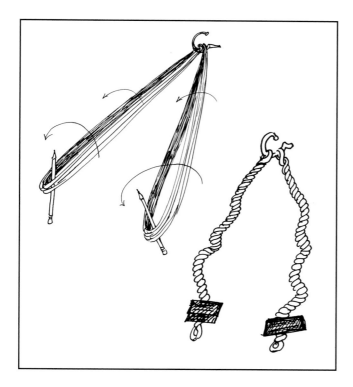

### *Try This!*

■ For a quicker method when twisting long cords, consider buying or making a rope machine. With coat hangers and two boards, you will have unlimited, creative possibilities for producing miles of cords. See diagram below.

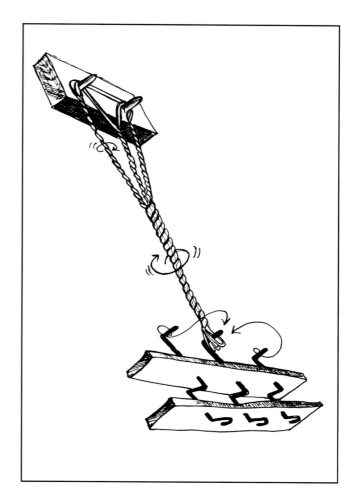

**Referring to the diagrams above:**

1. Loop lengths of fibers together, one for each section of the rope. Start with two to see how it works. Theoretically, any number of segments can be used.

2. Put lengths together and knot to form a loop. Anchor the loops securely with a weight or over a hook.

3. With your fingers, a pencil, a drill, an eggbeater, or a sewing machine, twist each loop until it kinks back on itself. Tape or pin the twisted loop to secure it while you work the next loop. Each loop can be a different fiber. Wind each loop in the same direction.

4. When all segments are twisted, pick them all up and twist together in the opposite direction. Knot at both ends to secure the rope.

■ A simple device for winding thin fibers can be constructed from a paper clip and a piece of cardboard or Styrofoam™. Elaborate on this winder using heavier wire and a wooden holder. It replaces the pencil and is one section of the rope machine. See diagrams below.

■ To achieve the effect of multiple cords without actually having to wind as many, wind off the fibers for one loop and then wrap contrasting threads around that loop. Put all the ends together and twist. This makes one segment. Make at least one more loop (plain or with a wrapped yarn), then twist together to form a cord.

■ Add additional cords to a completed rope. For instance, place a commercial, gold gift-wrap cord between the grooves of your hand-made rope by slightly untwisting each one, combining them, and twisting them together to fit. See diagram below.

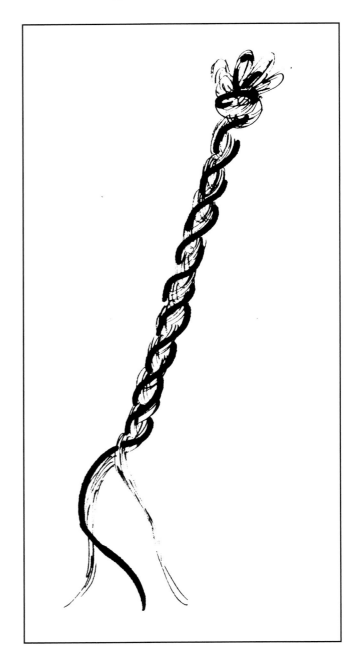

■ Normally, the loops of fibers to be twisted are the same length. If one is considerably longer than the others, it will randomly add loops and texture as it is twisted back into the group of cords. You may want to experiment with an uneven number of twists in each cord.

■ Commercial cords are often made by mechanically wrapping long lengths of fibers over a base core. Three or more of these cords are then plied together. To wrap your own in this manner, begin with a wide group of covering fibers. Winding a selection of threads on a ball winder, warping board, or C clamps will help this time-consuming process. Use upholstery cording or any old rope or cord you have handy as the core. Since it will be covered, the underlying core need only be the correct diameter. Wrap the core with fibers. If the core material has been spun, wrap it in the direction of the spin so the core doesn't unwind. If you have miles to cover, it is well worth attaching the core to a swivel, such as those found in a fishing store. Attach the swivel to a stationary object that you can pull against. This arrangement will turn the core as you concentrate on keeping the wrapping neat and tight. When the cord is covered, tape or overwrap the ends to secure. See diagram below.

■ A spinning wheel with a large orifice is a quick way to cover a thin core. Core-spinning with luscious fibers over a base fiber produces an elegant cord.

■ Once twisted, there are many things that can be done with a cord or rope. See illustrations below.

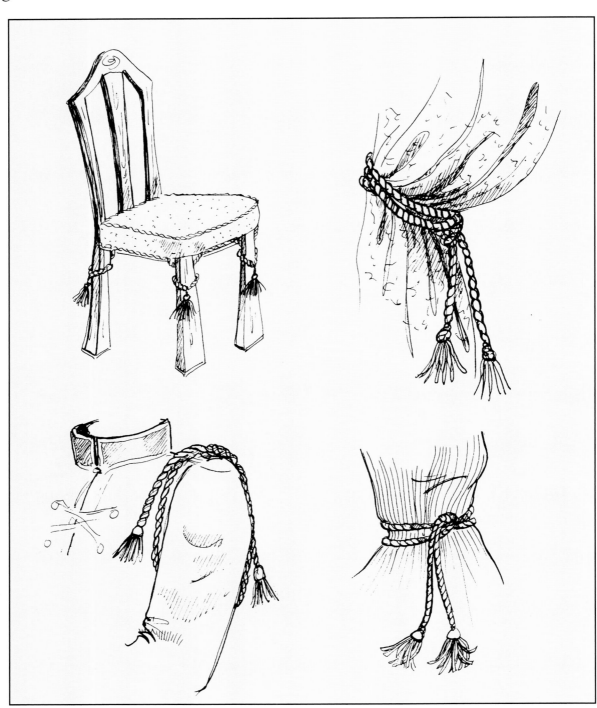

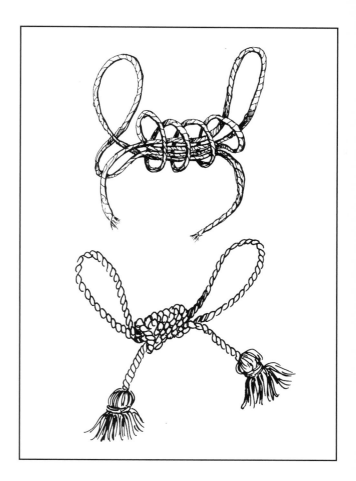

## MAKING DRAPERY TIEBACK CORDS

Perhaps the ultimate cord is the drapery tieback cord. These long, thick, twisted cords are joined to the tassel with a covered mold or a knot. Remember the green velvet costume worn by Vivian Leigh in *Gone with the Wind?* It was made from draperies with tiebacks and tassels holding it all together.

Referring to the diagrams above:

1. Attach the loop ends of the tieback to a wall or window frame. The knotted section with tassels attached is the center dimension. Measure to determine your decorating needs. Thick draperies will take up a bit more length. If you just want to give it a try without being too precise, start with 2½ yards of ½"-thick cord.

2. Leave a short end; form a 15" loop with the other end.

3. Loosely wrap over the double cord four times. The last wrap goes under and through the others.

4. Make another 15" loop on the other side, then pass the end through all the wraps again. Adjust the two ends as you tighten the knot. Insert both ends into a tassel.

## Try This!

■ Some tiebacks are constructed over a string core which is covered with fine threads or fabric. See illustrations at right.

■ If for any reason your cords turn out less than perfect, cover them with a sheer fabric to create elegance. The fabric can even have a slight pattern in it.

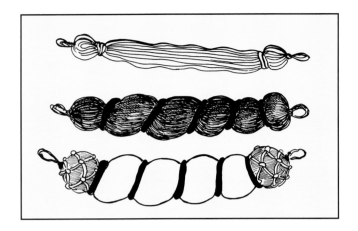

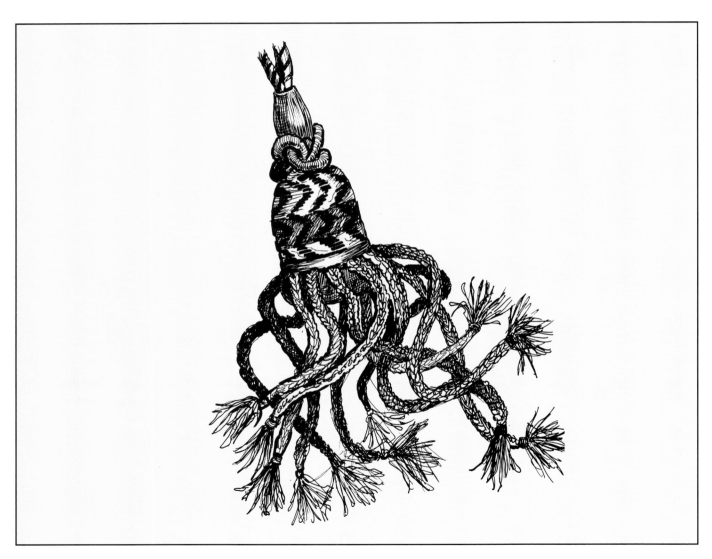

## MAKING A SPOOL-KNITTED CORD

A simple cord made on a knitting spool makes a nice design element stitched to the head or neck of a tassel. You may remember using a spool as a child. They are available in variety and toy stores, or you can make your own by hammering finishing nails in the end of a cylinder, such as a wooden thread spool. You will need a lifting device — a small knitting needle, a heavy toothpick, or even a paper clip will do. Spool knitting isn't fast, but it is simple and a good way to use up odds and ends of thread and yarn. See large illustration on page 26.

The thickness of the cord is determined by the number and spacing of the nails as well as the size of the spool. Any round object with prongs and a hole in the center makes a suitable knitting spool. A simple one is diagrammed, but feel free to experiment. See diagram below.

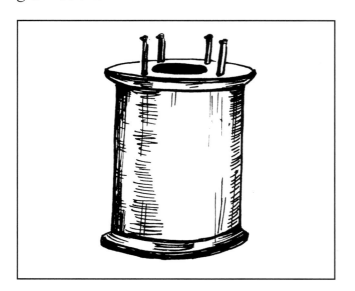

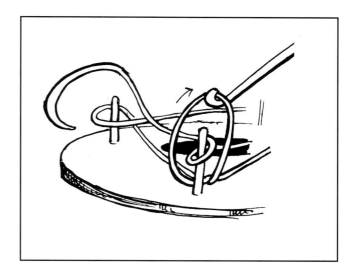

Referring to the diagram above:

1. To make a round cord, drop the end of the thread through the hole in the top of the spool, then loop it counterclockwise around each nail.

2. Hold the spool in your dominate hand and run the thread around the outside of the first nail.

3. With the lifting device, hook the original loop up and over the thread and drop it behind the nail. Gently tug on the end of the strand below the spool to tighten the stitch.

4. Turn the spool counterclockwise, lay the thread just above the second loop, lift the loop up over the thread, and nail and drop it behind.

5. When the cord is the desired length, place the last loop you made onto the nail next to it. Pick up the bottom loop, slip it over that loop, and drop it off the nail completely. Continue putting the remaining loops to the left and casting off. Run the yarn end through the last loop on the spool.

6. Remove the cord and pull the yarn tight. Take a few stitches to secure the end and the cord is complete.

■ Make a square cord by looping the yarn counterclockwise around each peg. Lift the old yarn over the cross made by the counterclockwise twist.

■ Either square or round cords can be knitted. See illustrations below.

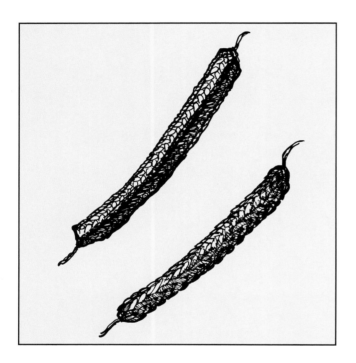

■ To add new colors and interesting textures, double the old and new ends for one complete round. Pull these double stitches tightly to prevent thickening.

■ Spool knitting can be used as a holding cord, but it stretches. To combat this tendency, try braiding lengths together. To stabilize it completely, insert a nonstretchy cord down the hole of the spool and work the knitting over it, then attach the tassel to the inside cord.

## MAKING A KNOTTED CORD

Knots enhance both the holding cords and the heads of tassels. Don't be afraid to experiment with knots and don't overlook the simplest ones. Use yarns, commercial cords, or cords you have made for tieing knots. Use knots alone or in a combination to add interest and diversity.

*Try This!*

■ Flat knots are easier to tie if they are first pinned to a board. Once woven, they are pulled up evenly and snugly before removing the pins.

■ Tie overhand knots, one on top of the other, to make a sturdy cord.

■ Tie knots with elasticized cord.

■ Try placing knots anywhere on the tassel. See illustration below.

*This commercial tassel of Korean origin shows knots on a holding cord.*

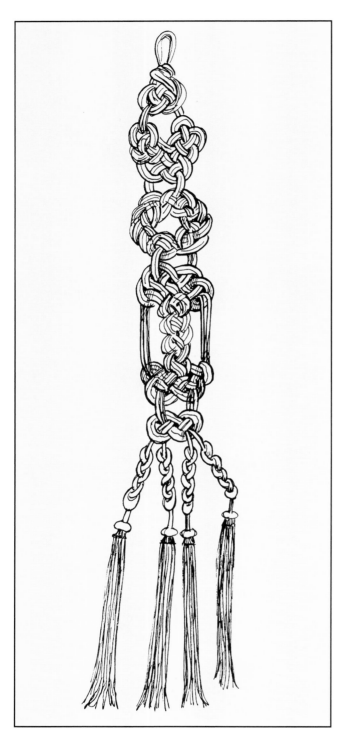

*Chinese tassels are usually simply constructed, relying on elaborately knotted holding cords for impact.*

■ A Keman-Musubi, or Japanese Buddist knot, starts with a double cord with loops drawn through from each side. See diagrams below.

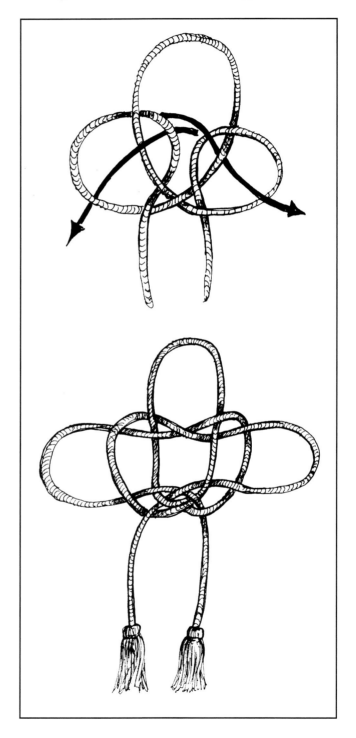

■ The knot diagrams on pages 31–33 are shown using one strand; however, working with two strands produces a richer-looking knot.

## Cloverleaf Knot

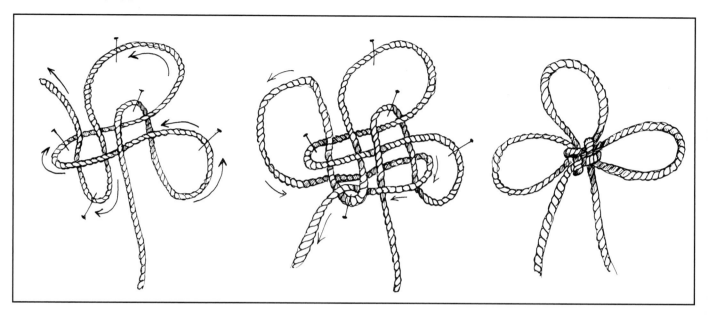

## Button Knot

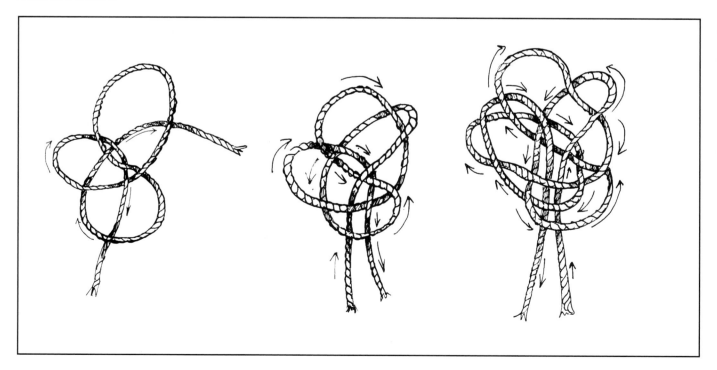

## Chinese Flat Knot

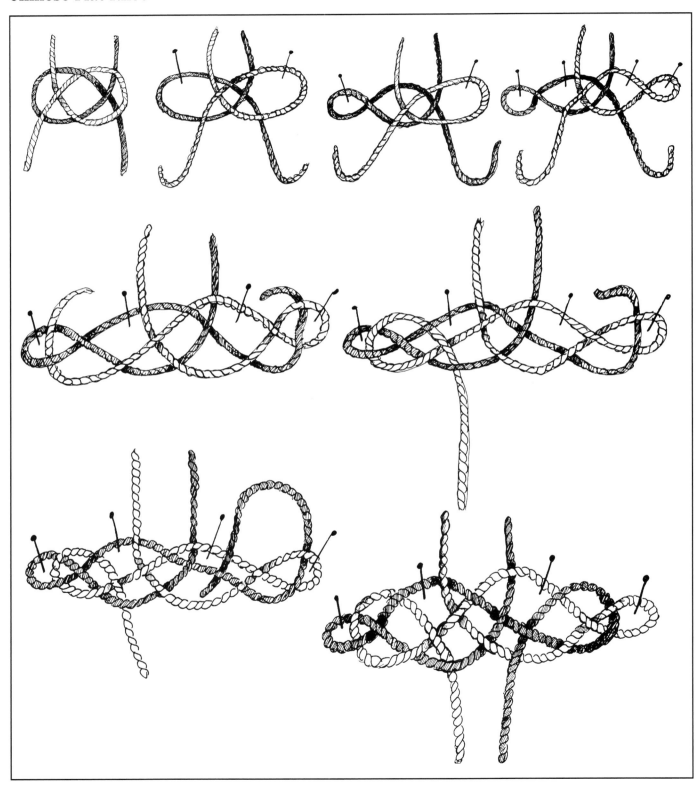

## Good Luck Knot

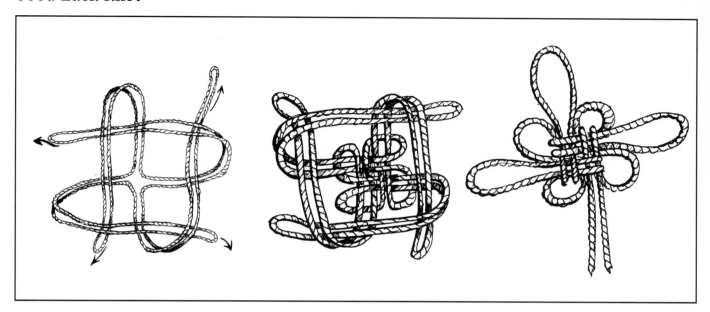

■ Knot a group of yarns together at the center to form a wonderful tassel head. See diagrams below.

■ Knot two or more colors to form a tassel head. See illustration below.

■ To attach knots to garments, manipulate them so the backs are smooth and the fronts are rounded.

*Afgani tassels are attached along the length of colorfully wrapped and twisted cords. Beads and metallic threads are added and the skirts are made of dozens of twisted strands often with seed beads incorporated in the ends.*

34

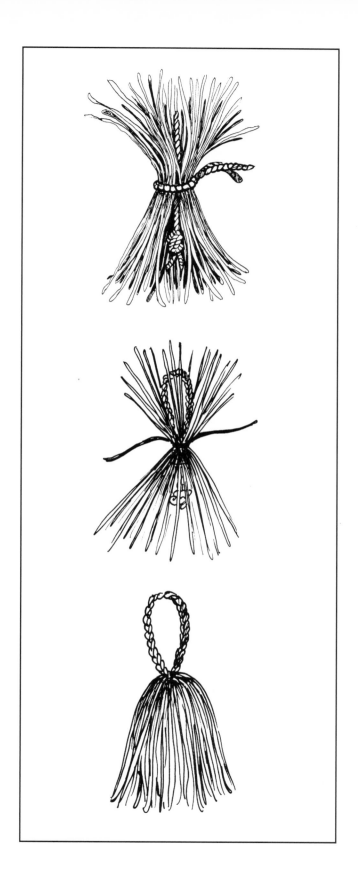

## CONNECTING THE BODY AND THE CORD

Tassels and their cords have to survive fondling, tugging, and pulling, so they must be securely connected. Knots or decorative molds may be added to the cord before connecting it to the tassel.

**Referring to the diagrams at left:**

**1. To connect the cord to the tassel, lay the twisted cord in the middle of and parallel to the tassel fibers; put the cord knot well below the center of the fibers.**

**2. Tie in the middle with a strong thread, bringing the tassel fibers up and around the cord.**

**3. Lift up the cord and let the fibers drape around the cord. This works just as well with a doubled cord.**

**4. Smooth the fibers, then wrap the tassel neck.**

**Referring to the diagram below:**

**1. As an alternative way to connect the cord to the tassel, place yarns through the twisted opening of the cord; then wrap the tassel neck.**

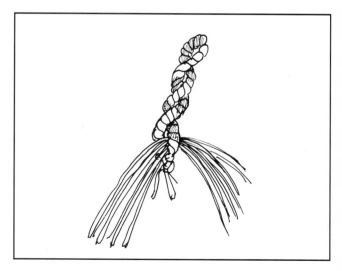

## Try This!

■ Construct a tassel on a ring rather than a cord by simply putting the yarns through and wrapping the neck.

■ Use a lark's head knot to attach yarns to rings or belt buckles.

■ The Ojibwa Indians attached tassels to braided buffalo leather instead of a cord. Loop the tassel yarns through the knotted end of a cord, fold them back over the knot, secure them to the cord, and, finally, fold and wrap again to make a smooth, finished head. If desired, add a bead. See illustrations below.

## WRAPPING THE NECK

Once you've wound the tassel and attached a cord, they must be secured in some sort of orderly fashion. Wrapping is the most versatile means to that end. Strong, smooth yarns work best. You will also need a large-eyed needle or a short sturdy loop of string or yarn.

**Referring to the diagram above:**

**1. Start the wrapping by laying one end of the chosen strands parallel to the tassel fibers and slightly below the area you want to wrap. Pinch this end with your thumb and take two or three turns at the top of the neck area to cinch it and all the tassel yarns.**

**2. Lay the needle with the eye pointed down below the area to be bound.**

**3. Wrap neatly over it for the neck length, then put the finished end into the loop or eye, pull up, and the ends are secured. Clip ends even with wrapping.**

### Try This!

■ If the tassel seems a bit soft-headed, insert a round or cylindrical bead into the top to alter the shape. See diagram below.

■ The head and neck provide hiding places for ends of yarn, knots, or special wishes. See illustration below.

### FINISHING THE BASIC TASSEL

When trimming the ends of the skirt, be as creative or precise as you like. Hold the tassel ends between your index and middle fingers and cut across, round up slightly on both ends to give a buoyant flair, or clip asymmetrically for a modern look.

With the neck wrapped and the bottom trimmed, you've got it all together in a basic tassel.

### Try This!

■ Barbara Leet designed a "ho-ho" to trim the bottom of her tassels as evenly as possible. She pulls her completed tassel inside a paper or PVC tube until just the ends are exposed and cuts them off even with the bottom of the tube. She has a drawer full of different sizes. She says not to bother trying to explain to the clerk at the hardware store why you want four-inch pieces cut from pipe that is normally sold in ten-foot lengths. That's why she calls it a "ho-ho."

■ Leave the bottom of a tassel uncut, retaining the loops. This is especially practical for a garment that will be washed, as the ends won't fray.

■ To smooth rumpled tassels, hold them over steam (use a fork to protect your hands) or comb them lightly with a blunt comb.

# TASSEL
## EMBELLISHMENTS

### DRESSING UP THOSE TASSELS

Once your basic tassel has been made, the fun really begins. When embellishing, let your imagination run wild. This provides a chance to try out new combinations and to experiment without commitment.

*Created by Gerda Rasmussen*

*Created by Gerda Rasmussen*

We all love to play dress up — and tassels love to dress up, too. Nothing is too silly to try — can you imagine the fun Greta Rasmussen had dressing the 24″ tassels shown in the photos on this page and on page 40.

39

## GATHERING DECORATIVE ACCESSORIES

Scoop all those little buttons, bolts, beads, bottle caps, washers, and what-nots that collect in corners of drawers and place them into a "dress up" box. Get out your old costume jewelry, gather up odds and ends, bits and pieces, rick-rack, and sequins — just as you did as a child. Bits of lace, ribbons, and string "too short to save" may come in handy on a tassel — another justification for never throwing anything away! When you have assembled your treasures, dress-up your tassel.

40

*Anything goes when dressing up a tassel.*

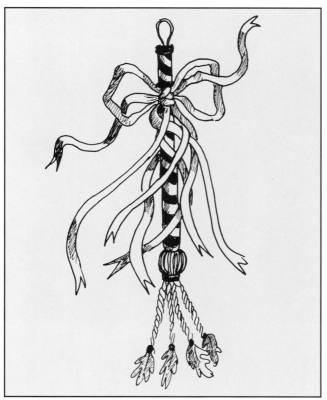

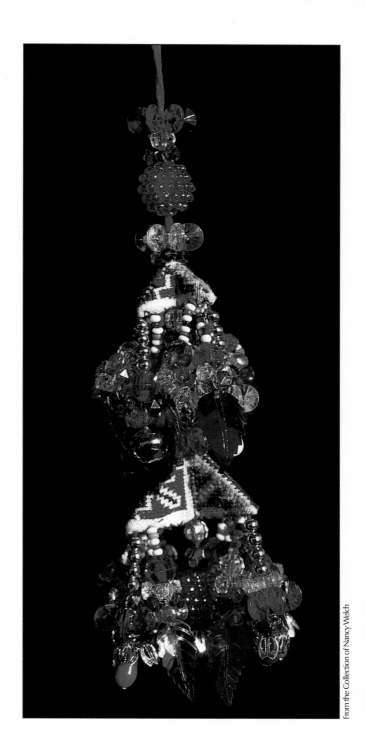

Have fun when embellishing tassels.
Make them come to life with
sound or light or texture.
See illustrations at left and photo above.

*Liz Turner Diehl dresses her tassel collection in cross-stitch and canvas work. Many of her tassel designs are then used on needlepoint pillows.*

## TASSEL TRUMPERY

Whatever technique is your specialty or whatever technique you have been wanting to try may prove perfect for a tassel: canvas work, counted thread, surface design, hand-dyed yarns, silk or metal embroidery, weaving, even handmade paper, will outfit any tassel.

### *Try This!*

■ Use beads, bells, bits of metal, or shells, not just for looks, but to add an element of sound. Mexican tin or shisha mirrors add sparkle. See illustration below.

■ For a touch of fragrance, wrap potpourri in a tiny packet and tuck it inside the head of a tassel. For a bolder statement, make a pomander ball by sticking cloves in an orange and using it for the head. Or, go all out and make a seed tassel for the birds out of an orange, bamboo leaves, millet, cloves, and twigs and grasses. See illustration below.

■ Buttons are used on Middle Eastern tassels to protect against the "evil eye." Try sewing them on with seed beads.

■ Hand-tack a piece of fabric, braid, or trim around the neck. (A zigzag stitch will reduce puckering.) If the ends are ragged, fold under a small seam allowance on each side, butt the two together, and use an invisible ladder or doll maker's stitch to connect them. See diagram below.

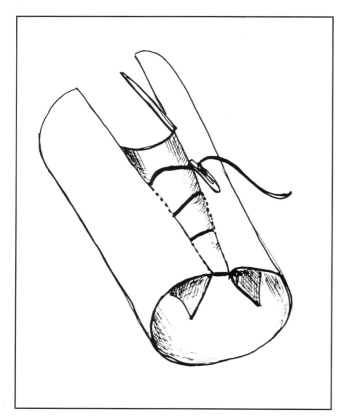

■ Weave ribbon, rattail cord, rick-rack, or a string of pearls into the first layer of trim.

■ Add glitz with sequins. They come in large and small flat disks, domed cup shapes, paillettes with holes in the side, and all sorts of fancy shapes and sizes including appliquéd designs.

■ Wrap lengths of wire or cover it by zigzagging over it with a sewing machine. Make spirals by wrapping wire around a knitting needle, or roll it into decorative shapes.

■ Embellish a tassel with swags of baby tassels. Lay cut ends over a long cord and wrap to form individual tassels. Gather the cord to form loops to tack wherever you like. Think of all the other places this can go! See diagram below.

■ Explore metallic yarns and other glitz, such as tinsel.

■ Make a Japanese form for your tassel to ripple from. Use decorative paper or weave a colorful thread pattern over the form. See diagrams and illustration below.

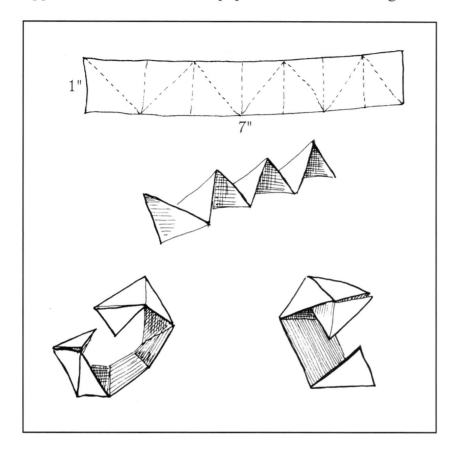

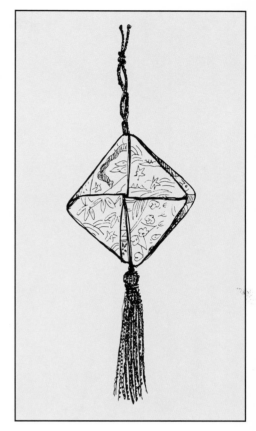

■ Trim tassels into exotic shapes. See illustrations below.

Created by Pennye Kurtela

Created by Marie Q. Sims

**Can't think of what to do
with all these creations?
Trim a basket or
handbag with tassels
as shown in the photos
on this page and on page 47.**

## WRAPPING FOR COLOR AND TEXTURE

Simple tassels can be set apart by elegant wrapping. Because wrapping is a construction necessity, basic wrapping has previously been explained on pages 36 and 37, but wrapping can do much more than just form a neck. Any part of a tassel can be wrapped. Experiment with color formulas.

### *Try This!*

■ Mix warm and cool colors, then blend them with a neutral color.

■ Use split-complementaries in unequal amounts.

■ Combine all dull or all bright colors.

■ Use one color in every conceivable texture and shade.

■ Match yarns to a favorite print fabric.

■ Copy colors from your favorite flower or leaf — you'll notice they are made up of several different shades and tints.

■ Use your eye to aim for a balanced color scheme or to create the most intense color texture possible.

■ Wrap with a variegated or space-dyed yarn for a quick and easy multicolored effect.

■ Hold two strands of differently colored fibers and wind them carefully side by side to form narrow stripes.

■ Form wide stripes by wrapping first with one color and then with another. Start at the top and work downward. Wrap over the end of the first color to secure. Both ends remain parallel to the tassel threads. This allows heavy textured fibers, weak fibers, and stiff materials like wire and leather to be used because they don't have to be pulled through the wrapped area. They are simply trapped inside the previous row. See illustration at left.

Created by Denise Hanlon

*Simple wrapping with a simple embellishment adds elegance to a linen tassel.*

■ Beads can be threaded onto the wrapping yarn, or they can be carried on an extra thread under the wrapping, and placed as needed. See diagram below.

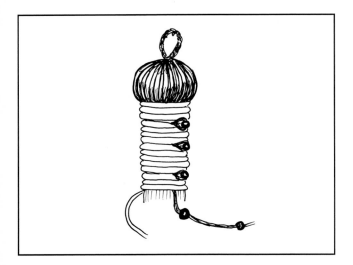

■ A decorative piece of yarn or ribbon can be placed under the wrapping and pulled to the surface to add texture. See diagram below.

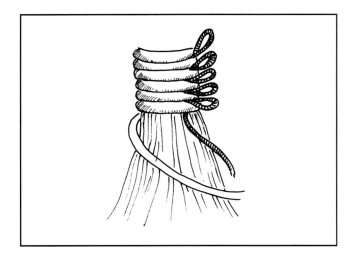

■ Stitch a circle of seed beads over a simple wrapping.

■ Add extra flair to the neck by wrapping a short ways, then dividing the tassel yarns into sections. Twist each section to make it puff out and form a kind of ruffle, wrap below the ruffle to anchor the twists. See diagram below.

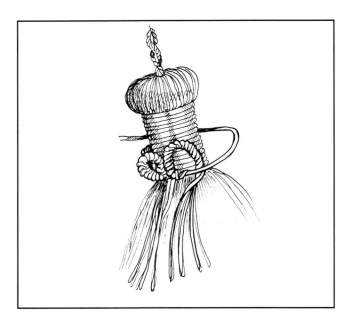

■ If you want to wrap long areas, the wrapping yarn tension can be controlled with your foot and the core material rolled along to cover quickly. Or, try the coffee cup and book approach. If you are wrapping with thread on a spool, stick the spool in a clean coffee cup, thread the end through a heavy book, and the tension is under control. If the wrapping yarn is on a skein that won't roll away from you, fill the coffee cup with your favorite beverage, place the yarn in the book and wrap leisurely.

## WRAPPING FOR SHAPE

Normally, a small area below the head of a tassel is wrapped to form a neck. However, doing something out of the norm creates interest and character.

### *Try This!*

■ Wrap all the way to the top and do away with the neck, or wrap all the way to the bottom and just leave a flouncy skirt. Unlike some figures, it is just fine for a tassel to be as wide as it is tall.

■ Create vertical stripes by changing colors or try leaving some areas unwrapped.

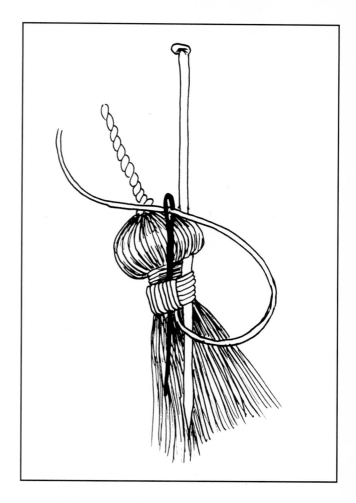

**Referring to the diagram above:**

**1.  To make yarn beads, loosely wrap a thick ring of yarn horizontally around the area to be embellished. Insert a thin pencil or a knitting needle to provide space for the wrapping.**

**2.  With a threaded needle, wrap vertically over the ring, compressing the horizontal yarns. The tighter the stitch, the harder and smaller the bead.**

**Gerda Rasmussen pulls sections of the vertical wrapping together in the center so the color of the horizontal wrapping shows through.**

*Wrap a ring for a holder, wrap sections for shaping, add charms, add tassels, and top it all off with a pompom.*

■ Wrap a loop at the top of the head to serve as a holder. See photo below.

Created by Ruthmarie Hofmann

■ Fat yarn beads add charm to tassels. See photo below.

Created by Jerry Zarbaugh

Created by Madge Copeland

■ Combine yarn beads and tassels to make necklaces. See photo above.

53

■ Wrap dozens of necks along the length of a large tassel. Wrap heavily in one area to form a "bump" or stuff padding under the wrapping for "lumps." If the padding is interesting, like fleece, let parts of it poke out.

■ If the wrapping doesn't please you, weave ribbons over it or cover with a decorative ribbon or fabric. See illustration below.

■ Wrap a group of threads in the center and twin tassels is the end result. See illustration below.

■ Wrapping is a quick way to provide almost any shape imaginable. Wrap and pad tops to create fanciful shapes. Add embellishments over the wrapped forms. See illustrations below.

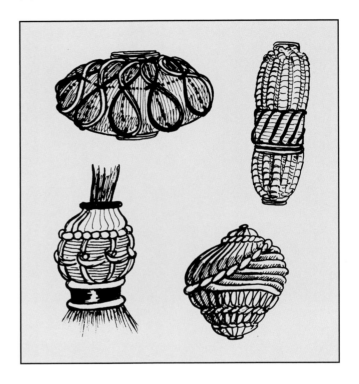

■ Divide and wrap the tassel to form figures. See illustration below.

Long wrapped necks form these slinky tassels.

*Yarn beads provide a foundation for real beads.*

## WRAPPING FOR A FOUNDATION

Neat wrapping provides a place to add your own touch of enrichment. Even if the wrapping isn't so neat, you can cover it with embroidery stitches, use it as a base for needle-weaving, or couch metallic threads over it. Sew on sequins, beads, buttons, or bells. If you crave instant gratification, simply stitch on a tiny circle of lace, ribbon, rick-rack, or embroidered trim.

### *Try This!*

■ Even the tiniest scraps of precious ribbons can dress-up a tassel.

■ Make a unique tassel for a friend by including special interest charms or alphabet beads to spell their name. See diagram below.

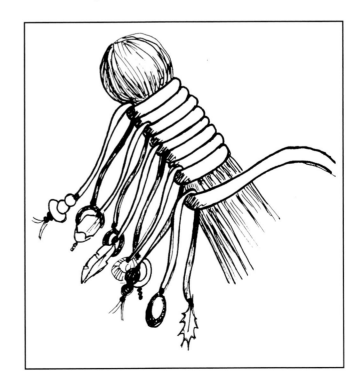

Created by Pat Goldstene

*Wrapping provides a foundation for adding embellishments such as bells.*

■ Wrap the head or neck "Chinese style" by pulling out sections of tassel threads to form a design as you wrap. See illustration below.

■ Add extra yarns and features to turn a tassel into a figure. See illustration below.

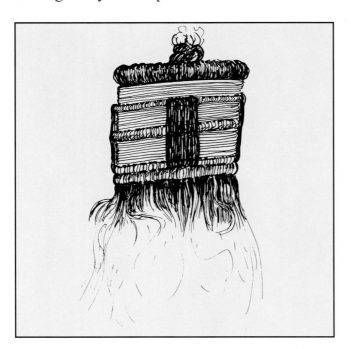

■  Work ribbon streamers or slim braids into the wrapping, progressing down its length. Include feathers, shells, and tiny treasures in the braids or dangle them from the streamers. See illustration below.

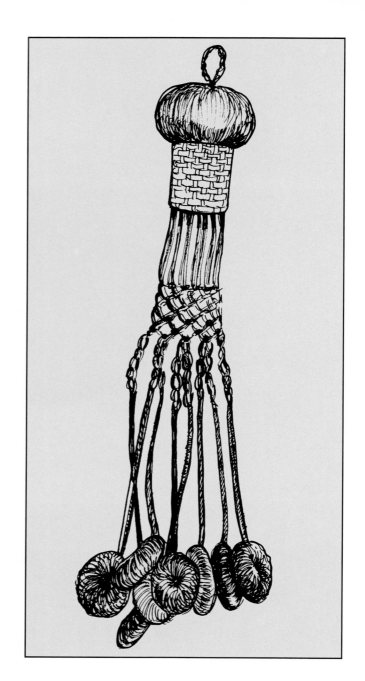

## ADDING LOOPS AND RINGS

Many ethnic tassels, especially those from the countries of India and Guatemala, incorporate colorful wrapped rings. Some rings are wrapped, others are buttonhole stitched.

*Uncovered jade rings act as weights on scroll tassels from China.*

## Try This!

■   Keep in mind that all loops and rings can be used to hang tassels. Any size ring, from a bracelet to a finger ring, covered or not, can be used. Antique napkin rings are delightful.

■   Washers, drapery rings, and cardboard tubes are other likely candidates for covering.

■   Make a ring of any diameter by winding a cord in a circle and wrapping it to secure the ends. See diagram below.

■   Wrap or use a buttonhole stitch to cover the ring. Try using several colors. See diagram below.

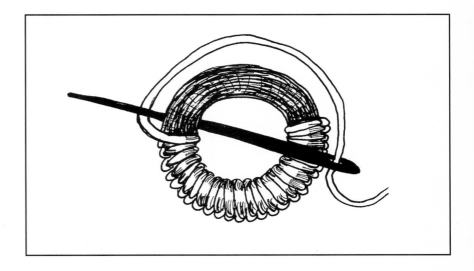

■　Add rings to the holding cord for interest. See illustrations below.

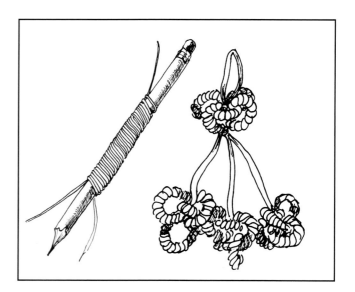

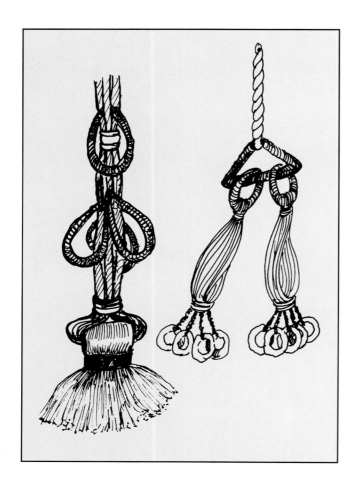

■　Use decorative rings around the head or neck, or hang a bunch on the skirt for added bounce and color.

■　Often found on Italian linens, these tassels are made by wrapping fibers around a pencil or rod to form a loop, then wrapping each of these little loops with more strands. The wrapped loops are formed into various configurations and are sometimes combined with knotted tassels. See diagrams at top right.

*Embellished rings serve as hangers for holiday tassels.*

*Rita Zerull needlelaces on rings to construct tassel earrings.*

**Referring to the diagram above:**

**1. To needleweave a tassel as shown in the photo at left, use a blunt-pointed tapestry needle to avoid splitting the fibers as you weave.**

**2. Just poke and pull — the ends will hide under base yarns.**

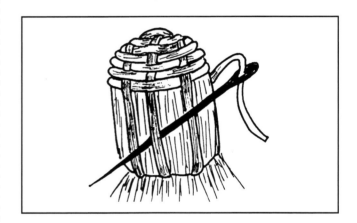

**Referring to the diagram above:**

**1. To needleweave a tassel, warp the head, neck, or a form (rags, wooden molds, etc.) with strong, firm threads to create a miniature loom for weaving patterns.**

**2. Thread a tapestry needle with the weft yarn. Start weaving at the top of the core. Weave the yarn over, under, over each warp in turn, on an uneven number of warps.**

## NEEDLEWEAVING

Needleweaving involves stitching or weaving extra yarns over base yarns. Tassel heads, wrapped sections, and yarn-covered molds are all just waiting for your threaded needle. Think of them as a blank canvas and the needle as the brush. Explore design possibilities.

### Try This!

■ For a raised, ridged effect, take the threaded needle under two warps and around one, then under two more warps, and around one. This is referred to as the Egyptian weave or the raised stem stitch. See diagram below.

■ To create a smooth padded look, weave over two warps and under one. This is referred to as the rib stitch. See diagram below.

■ Wrap each individual warp vertically for a bullion-stitch effect. See diagram below.

■ Work a chain stitch over the last row of warps as a finish. See diagram below.

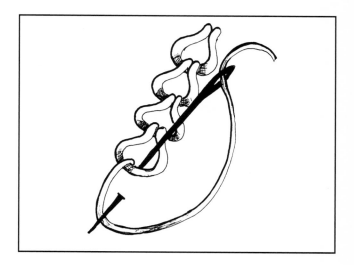

■ If you are a weaver, try twill or tapestry weaves.

**Referring to the diagrams at left:**

1. To needleweave a tassel on a flat surface, pin the warps on a foam core board in any shape that pleases you. Use tapestry needles to weave color, texture, and design on the warps.

2. Pack the yarns tightly with a fork. Insert beads and other trinkets directly onto the warps as you work.

3. Weave the lower part of the warps separately creating legs or leave free forming a skirt.

4. Roll the finished woven top to form a tubular head or attach to the neck.

5. If needed, more yarns can be added to fill out the skirt, using a lark's head knot.

## *Try This!*

■   Needleweave with everything from silk to raffia. Try strips of torn fabric.

■   Place warps anywhere on a tassel and needleweave with ribbons. When working with ribbon, keep it loose and twist it to achieve the effect you like. See diagram below.

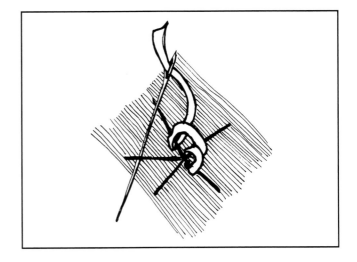

**Referring to the diagrams above:**

1. To needleweave a tassel head on a circular loom, construct a small loom from a cardboard circle. Start with a 3″ diameter.

2. Cut eight small slits evenly around the outside of the circle.

3. Warp back and forth around each slit on the top surface only to form spokes. Don't go across the bottom or you won't be able to remove the loom when finished.

4. Needleweave through the warps, changing colors if you wish, or weave a tapestry design on the loom.

5. Remove the loom. There will be two sides from which to choose. Draw up the woven circle by running a gathering thread around the outside edge.

6. Adjust the covering to fit over the head of a tassel. Stitch in place.

## WEAVING ON A LOOM

Karen Madigan shares her technique for weaving tassels on an inkle loom. Using an inkle loom is a great way to make a number of tassels at one time.

Imagine the possibilities for tassel head designs that a multiharness loom offers. European braids and fringes are made on looms set up so one section weaves the top band. A space is left unwarped, then a tight warp is placed to catch each weft pass and form the fringe.

To make many small tassels, set up strips of warp on a frame or floor loom. To use this technique as the neck, fold one section of the unwoven ends to the inside to form the head.

1. To weave a tassel on an inkle loom, thread the loom with 149 warp ends of 2/20 cotton. The weft is a tripled piece of warp material.

2. To start, leave 4″ unwoven. Weave seven rows of plain weft.

3. Weave a pick-up row of design or insert a tiny piece of frayed fabric for texture.

4. Weave six more rows, then another pattern row, and finish with eight plain rows.

5. Leave about 10″ of warp unwoven between each tassel for the skirts. When the warp is complete, cut the tassels apart in the middle of the 10″ section.

*Karen Madigan of Old Bar, Australia, uses an inkle loom to make tassel earrings with woven heads.*

**Referring to the diagrams at left:**

1.  Fold one edge over to double the number of threads in the tassel. Glue a few threads inside the tassel to form loops to which jewelry findings may be attached.

2.  Roll the tassel tightly and secure the ends with a needle and thread.

## CROCHETING

There is something for everyone in tassel making. Crochet is fast to do, and can be self-taught with the help of a good instruction book.

Crocheted tassel heads have long been popular. To make a head, single crochet a form and slip over a completed tassel or crochet directly over the tassel head. Start at the top and increase and decrease to fit.

To make crocheted spirals, make a chain the length of the bobble, then crochet back into each loop of the chain three times to form a curly spiral. You can single, double, or triple crochet back into the chain. Make a group to embellish or to form into a tassel.

Acorn shaped tassels with crocheted tops were popular in the 1920s. See illustration below.

From the Collection of Margery Williams

## SHISHA MIRROR EMBROIDERING

Shisha mirrors from India lend sparkle to any tassel. The traditional way to add them is to make a thread frame over the mirror and do a decorative stitch around the outside to secure it to the background. See diagrams below.

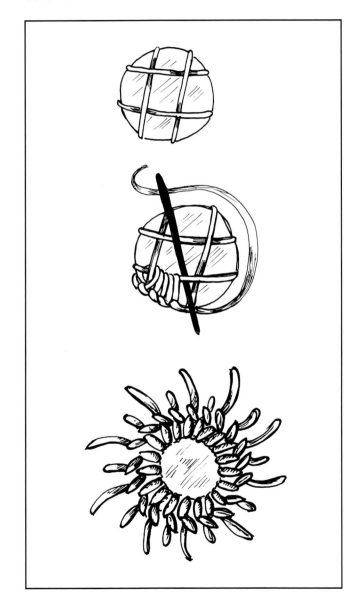

## Try This!

■ For an easy variation, wrap over a loop or plastic ring, place that over the mirror, and stitch it to the tassel.

■ Substitute large colored sequins for shisha mirrors. See illustration below.

## USING EMBROIDERY

Just about any kind of stitch can go just about anywhere on a tassel. Add beads or other embellishments to the stitching thread and work in as you go along.

The type of threads you use will greatly affect the final result. Try an array of materials: rayon embroidery floss, hand-dyed silk threads or ribbons, metallics, perle cotton with a nice sheen, or whatever else you have in your special stash!

### Buttonhole Stitching

This versatile stitch can face up or down and be worked right to left or left to right. In macramé, it's called a half hitch, weavers call it knotless netting, Scandinavians call it nalbinding, Australians have yet another name for it. You may soon call it the only stitch you need to know. It's as easy as writing an "e." See diagram below.

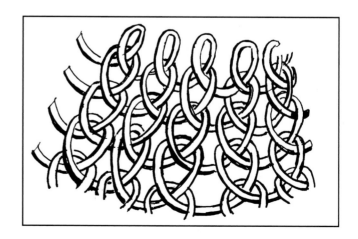

Try it attached or detached, open and loose, or worked tightly to completely cover an area. Let the stitch meander about in many colors or be controlled to form a pattern. See illustration below.

## Blanket Stitching

This is an attached buttonhole stitch. See diagram below.

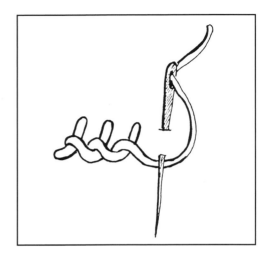

## Couching

This stitch is useful for thick or metal fibers that can't be sewn directly. See diagram below.

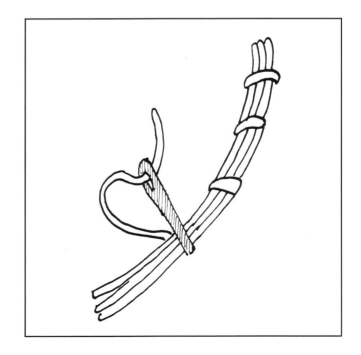

*Vima embellishes a group of colorful tassels with the buttonhole stitch.*

## French Knot

The French knot is a very popular stitch and can also be stitched with a stem. See diagrams below.

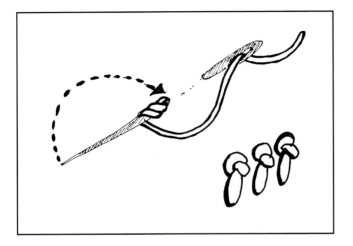

## Bullion Knot

These knots are great to shape and bend, wiggle, and squiggle around the neck of any tassel. See diagram below.

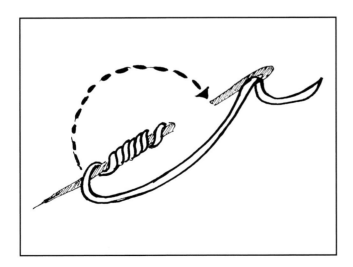

## Herringbone Stitching

When made close together, these stitches form a decorative braid. See diagrams below.

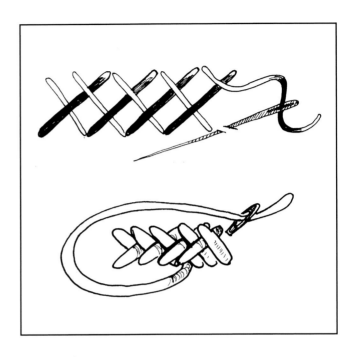

## Zigzag Braiding

Using a thick, smooth yarn gives the look of an expensive commercial trim. See diagrams below.

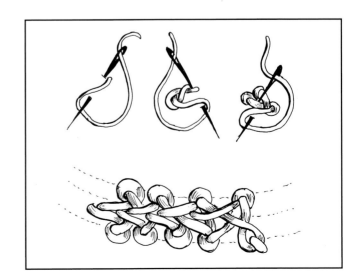

Created by Alix Peshette

*Yarn beads and French knots liven up this group of tassels that Alix Peshette made for her horse.*

*Stitchery embellishes
a pendant and
yarn covered
cork bead
to set off
a small tassel.*

74

## Chain Variation and Picot Edging

These techniques make nice finishing edges and beads look great dangling from the loops. See diagrams below.

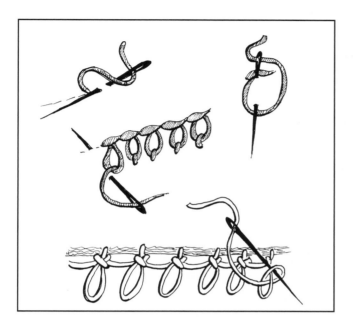

### *Try This!*

■ To make dimensional shapes, use silk ribbons to form the stitches.

■ Make a net of buttonhole stitches over a tassel head. See illustration below.

■ Stitch with strips of fabric or pull them through the loose yarns of a wrapped area. Experiment with velvet, taffeta, moiré, organza, and other fine fabrics. Give a try to knits and anything else that may be lying around. The effects are often delightful.

■ Work a buttonhole stitch over a ring to make a hanger, or buttonhole stitch over the hanging cord itself to add substance.

■ Use closely spaced stitches to hold precious objects or to form secret hiding spaces. See illustration below.

*Jett Thorson collects antique flowers, stamens, beads, leaves, and wires to add to her handmade silk flowers on her elegant hand-dyed rayon tassels.*

## EMBELLISHING WITH FLOWERS

Flowers are fun to make and are an especially wonderful embellishment for wedding, shower, and baby tassels.

During Louis XV's reign, French tassels were embellished with small ornamental rosettes or loops (jasmins) made by wrapping silk threads over metal forms. Sometimes the entire skirt would be made of rosettes. In the early twentieth century, French designer Poiret fashioned nosegays of fabric flowers into tassels. While you probably won't find many tassels from Louis XV's reign, keep an eye out for antique flowers, ribbons, trims, and beads. A tiny bit will have a big impact on an ordinary tassel.

Today it's easier to make flowers with ribbons. Glorious, wired French ribbons form fabulous flowers with just a twist. Less expensive satin ribbons makes nice roses, albeit with a bit more work.

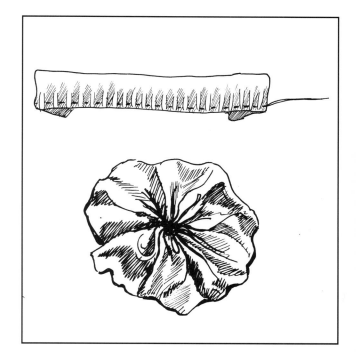

**Referring to the diagrams above:**

**1. To make an open flower, gather a rectangular piece of ribbon along one edge with the ends turned under.**

**2. Pull the gathers in a circle to create an open flower.**

Referring to the diagram below:

1.  To make a sewn flower on a form, first you must make a form to wind the ribbon around. A coat hanger or sturdy wire bent into a "U" shape is used to slip under your sewing machine needle for stitching. A more versatile device can be made by drilling holes at various distances in a narrow piece of wood with two dowels or rods extending so the ribbon can be wrapped in wider folds. This is useful for winding tassels, pompoms, and ruching.

2.  Wind ribbon, seam binding tape, yarn, or a mixture, around the rods.

3.  Sew about 1" or so from one edge to make fringe. Remove from form.

4.  Roll the fringe into a tassel, wrap a neck (or tie a bow with the ribbon) to cover the stitching, and let the short end fall over to form the top. It looks a little like a shaggy flower.

5.  Cut the long end of the fringe or leave in loops for the skirt. Before rolling, insert a cord for hanging if desired.

NOTE: Experiment with the proportions for unique effects.

Referring to the diagram at right:

1.  To make a sewn flower, fold a wide ribbon zigzag fashion and sew down the center.

2.  Bend the length in half along the seam and roll to form a rose-shaped flower.

3.  After folding, stitch through all the layers to secure.

NOTE: It takes about two yards of $^7/_8$"-wide ribbon to make a nice full flower. Experiment with the space between the zigzags to make loose or compact flowers.

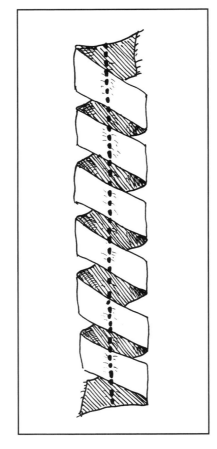

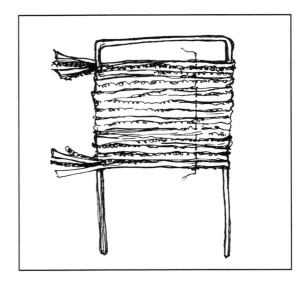

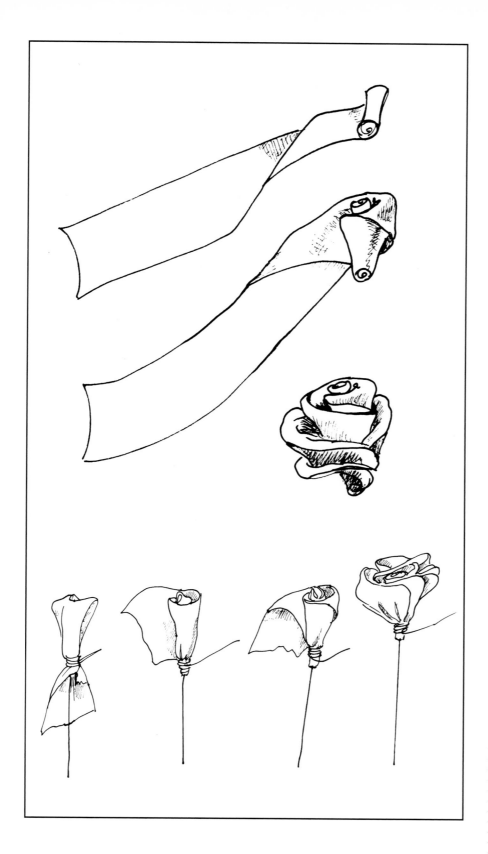

Referring to the diagrams at left:

1. To make a basic rose, start by rolling one end of a ribbon into a tight tube to form a center.

2. Diagonally fold the ribbon away from you on the top edge and roll the center along the fold to the end. This makes a cone around the tube.

3. Fold diagonally again and roll to the end of that fold. Each fold makes a petal.

4. Wire or stitch the ends as you work. Shape the flower by making the top a little wider with each turn.

5. If a stem is desired, fold one end of the ribbon over at the top and shape the ribbon into a flower directly on the stem.

NOTE: The width of the ribbon determines the size of the rose. The wider the ribbon, the more length is needed. A yard of $1^1/_2''$ ribbon makes a generous flower. Half a yard of $1''$ ribbon is sufficient.

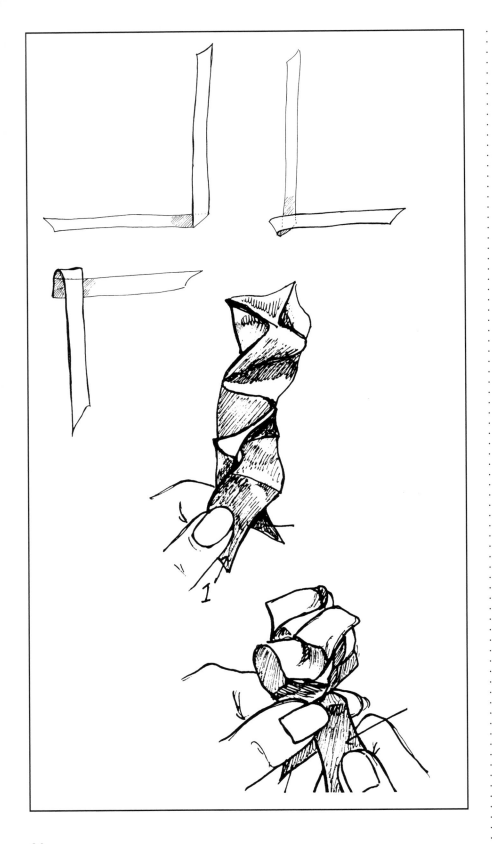

Referring to the diagrams at right:

1. To make a quick-folded rose, diagonally fold a piece of ribbon in half to form a right angle.

2. Fold the alternating ends back and forth into neat accordion-pleated squares, one on top of the other. Make at least twelve folds.

3. Hold the last fold and pull down gently on the underneath end to squish-up the folds and form a flower.

4. Wire or stitch the ends securely. Take a couple of stitches through the center of the rose to secure it. Cut off the tail if desired. To avoid leaving a tail, keep the ribbon attached to the roll and make the last fold of ribbon with the cut end, then you'll be pulling on the end that is still connected to the roll.

**Referring to the diagrams below:**

1. **To make a jasmin, thoroughly wrap a 6" length of florist wire.**

2. **Bend the wire into a flower shape and you'll have an approximation of a French jasmin.**

3. **For a different look, wind the covered wire over a thin knitting needle, remove the needle, and bend into a "crinkle" jasmin.**

**NOTE: Jasmins are three-dimensional decorations formed over wire. Lengths of florist wire, especially the green type, are handy and easy to cover.**

## *Try This!*

■ Use any embroidery technique for adding dainty flowers directly to tassels.

■ Craft a cute, fat bud from a small tube of ribbon. Gather one side of a strip of ribbon just below the selvedge to form the top. Stuff it with cotton and gather the other side to close the tube. Some ribbons have a contrasting color edge which will highlight the little ruffle formed by the selvedge at the top. Since you aren't apt to be washing flowers or tassels, don't hesitate to add color as needed with the touch of a marker. See diagram below.

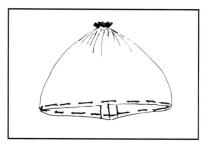

■ Form an even simpler bud from a scrap of precious ribbon by folding a square of wide ribbon in half diagonally and tightly binding all the cut edges with thin wire or stitch securely. Cover the wire or tuck it into the tassel neck as you work. See diagrams below.

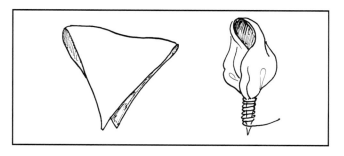

■ Make a leaf by folding a scrap of ribbon in half and gathering it below the fold. The width of the ribbon and the placement of the gathers determine the size of the leaf. Turn the leaf so the folded part is underneath before attaching it. See diagrams below.

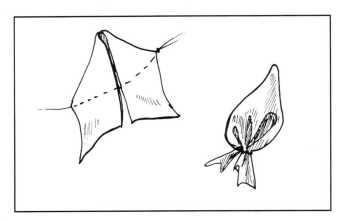

*A Chinese batik fabric tassel.*

## USING FABRICS

Obviously, making tassels is a marvelous way to use up left-over threads, fibers, and yarns, but these are not a requirement. Bits of fabric make unusual tassels, either used alone or with an additional fiber, such as yarn. Using fabrics for tassels is truly a dress-up technique. If the colors aren't compatible, overdye the finished tassel. The secret is to find a dye that will handle all the fibers you have used; be certain to thoroughly read the labels on the dyes.

*Small fabric tassels set off an elaborately knotted cord from Korea.*

## Try This!

■ Construct a tassel with decorative fabrics cut into strips and used like yarn. Roll the fabric and then slit.

■ Fold fabric "coats and skirts" to encase part or all of a tassel. See illustration below.

■ Make little ball tassels from fabric; add decorative knots. Buttonhole-stitch over the cord. See diagram below.

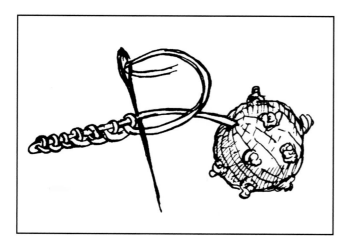

■ Stuff small circles or other shapes of muslin with batting. Add sweet-smelling herbs. Margo Carter Blair constructs a cone-shaped mold from heavy paper, covers it with yarn, and finally inserts feathers around all. As a final fillip, she adds beads or bells at the base of the muslin. See illustration below.

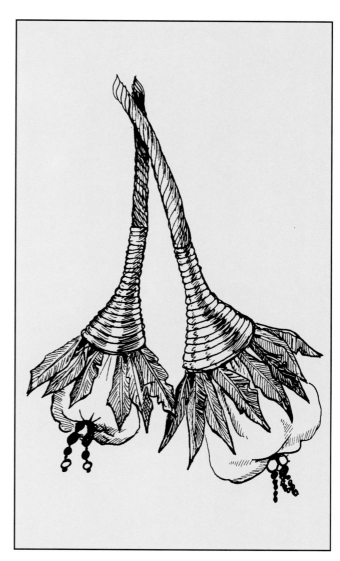

*These molds await their turn to be transformed with elegant threads at a tassel factory.*

# TASSEL
## MOLDS

### HARD-HEADED TASSELS

Early molds were formed by first making a flat model of the proposed structure and then constructing a cardboard tube the diameter of the smallest portion of the model to serve as a base. Strips of fabric were wrapped over this core to approximate the outline of the model. Thread was then bound on to refine the shape, and finally, a cloth covering was sewn on to cover the "skeleton." Over this framework, silk and metal cords were braided, wrapped, woven, and knotted to create an elaborate top for the tassel.

This time-consuming construction was later replaced by wooden forms turned on a lathe. Coverings are glued or worked directly over the wood. Various shapes are combined to create extraordinary configurations. Each form is individually covered, then threaded on a cord or an inner shaft, and a separate skirt added. The intricacy is remarkable!

Created by Catherine Coleman  Photo Courtesy of McCalls Needlework

Usually made of wood, molds come in all shapes and sizes and are often stacked to produce even more complex shapes. Covered molds are an integral part of formal European style tassels.

## MAKING YOUR OWN MOLDS

If commercial molds are unavailable, remember that folk tassels are made from whatever is at hand. Hunks of rag or hair take the place of fancy molds. If you take a peek up the skirt of any "fat" tassel, you never know what you might find. Perhaps my favorite is the light bulb; this mold substitution was used on a tassel I found in Timbuktu. See illustration below.

*The anatomy of an elegant tassel consists of stacking several molds together, covering each section of the body with fibers, then finishing it with a fringe skirt.*

## Try This!

■ Produce a shaped top with wrapping. Cording forms a mold quickly. See diagrams below.

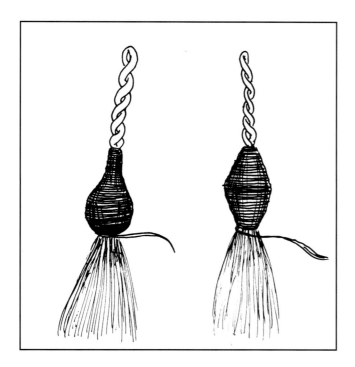

■ Carve shapes from Styrofoam™ or fishing corks, or contour the molds with cardboard and papier mâché. To add substance to these lighter materials, a lead weight can be added.

■ Form polymer clay into a mold or make it into a crowning glory for your tassel.

■ Cotton batting, covered with cloth, wrapping, or felt, makes decorative stitching and bead application easy.

■ Be creative when looking for molds. Wooden beads, empty thread spools, PVC pipe, wine and champagne bottle corks, and wrapping paper tubes are all mold substitution candidates. Styrofoam™ balls (covered or uncovered) can be used at the top of any cardboard tube. See illustration below.

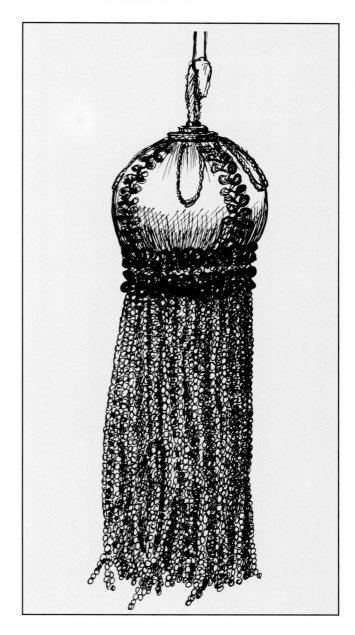

■ Imitate a Chinese tassel by draping silk threads (the length of the tassel) over a form to give the impression of a full tassel. Secure the silk threads by wrapping with metallic thread, leaving sections of the tassel threads exposed to form a design. See photo at right.

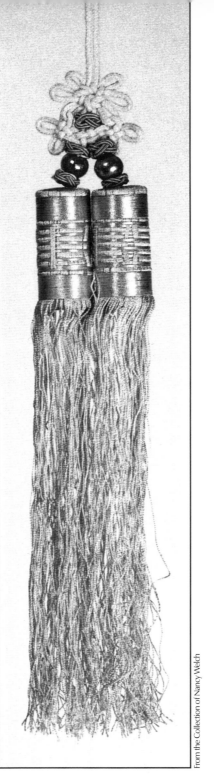

From the Collection of Nancy Welch

*Chinese tassels are usually made in pairs. Some pairs are joined at the mold.*

■ When using wooden molds, keep in mind they do not have to be "round." Square and rectangular blocks and beads make extraordinary molds for unusual tassels. See illustration below.

## COVERING MOLDS

Once you have a basic mold, determine the best way to cover it. The shape of the mold will help determine whether it should be wrapped horizontally or vertically.

*A collection of covered molds waiting to be strung into tassels at Merwitz Textiles in Chicago, Illinois.*

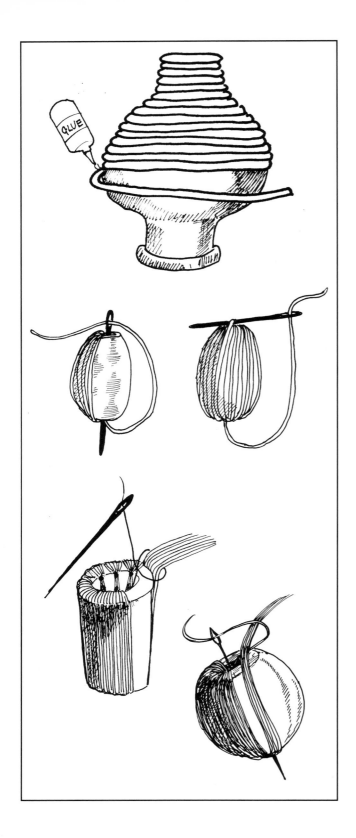

Referring to the diagrams at left:

1. The traditional way to cover a hard mold is to apply glue and then wrap the mold with the covering fibers. Coat the mold with a thin layer of white or fabric glue and let it set until tacky. If you are concerned about posterity, use archival quality glue.

To start, secure the end of the yarn, braid, gimp, or other covering to the inside of the mold. Putting the mold on a pencil or knitting needle makes it easier to turn, and keeps your fingers cleaner, while you are wrapping. Work slowly, pressing the covering firmly against the glue as you go. Keep the wraps as close together as possible so none of the mold shows through.

2. If the mold being covered has a large hole, wrap the fibers around the mold and through the hole. Fine threads, such as 150/2 rayon, make a smoother surface when making elegant tassels.

3. If the hole "fills up," continue covering the outside of the mold by taking small stitches through the top and bottom of the base fibers.

4. To make more room on the inside of the mold, group the covering fibers as you go to spread them on the outside.

5. Another trick is to use a sturdy sewing thread on the inside. Hook the thicker covering fibers just on the outside of the mold at both top and bottom. Catch clumps of fibers to speed things up. Pass the strands back and forth on the inside, looping around the covering fibers. Turn the covering fibers so they go up and down on the outside of the mold.

*These duplicate tassels from Scarlet O'Hara's dress in "Gone with the Wind" are covered with rayon thread, assembled with a netted cording, and small tassels applied over the bullion skirt.*

*Covering molds can be time-consuming, but the finished tassel is well worth the effort.*

## Try This!

- If the mold itself is pretty or you are feeling lazy, leave it exposed. Molds can be gilded, painted, or découpaged.

- The covered mold can be used as is or further embellished with ribbons, braids, or cords. To evenly distribute the trimmings, divide the mold into fourths with straight pins to act as a guide. It is easier to start at the top of the mold with the middle of the ribbons so you don't have ends to contend with at both the top and the bottom. More than one row of trimming can be added; but establish the pattern with the widest trim first and then add others. Stitch or glue the trimming in place. See diagram below.

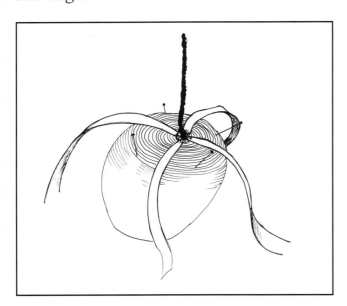

- Add decorative beads and buttons to create more fanciful shapes.

- Weave ribbons, braids, or cords over the wrapped molds.

- When covering molds with intricate designs and elaborate embellishments, oftentimes several straight pins are needed. See diagram below.

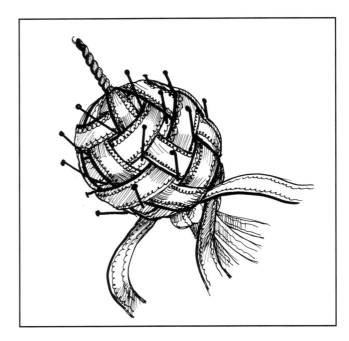

- String a few strands of glass beads over wooden beads to create a sparkly tassel top.

- Work detached buttonhole-stitched or crocheted coverings decoratively over a wrapping or directly over the mold as the only covering.

- Heavy tassel drapery weights are made by covering a lead mold with thread and then working a cord netting over the entire form.

- Try several types of covered mold shapes together (even flat cardboard) to form a neck or head for a tassel or to string on the cord.

## ADDING THE SKIRT

Once you have the basic mold covered, determine the type of fibers you want to attach as the skirt.

There are basically three methods for adding the skirt to your tassel.

Add yarns one at a time with a lark's head knot through the bottom yarns of the mold. A crochet hook is helpful. Work with clumps of yarn or the tassel may never get completed.

Hand- or machine-stitch along the top of the loose yarns to form a "wrap-around" skirt. Glue or wire the skirt to the mold.

Knot the tassel yarns together with a separate strong thread along the top of the form as they are wound.

*Sometimes you may find a mold that doesn't require covering.*

From the Collection of Nancy Welch

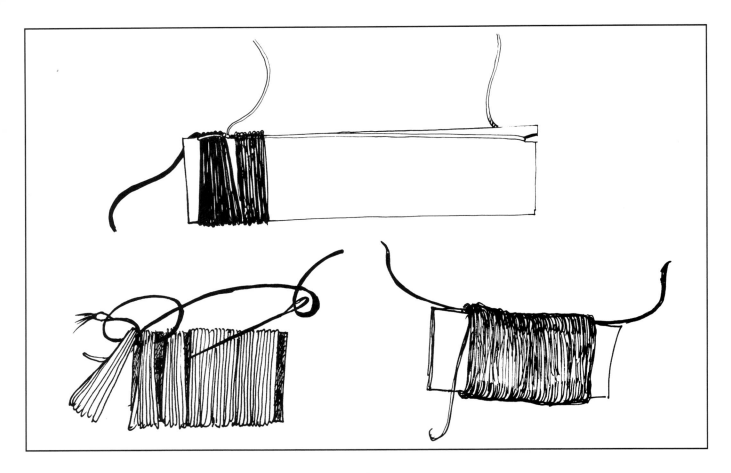

Ceramic Molds Designed by MacKenzie-Childs, Ltd.

Referring to the diagrams above:

1. Wind fibers a few times, tie a knot with thread, wind some more, and tie those together. Continue until the skirt is wide enough to go around the bottom of the mold.

2. For a thicker skirt, wind fibers over each other before tieing the knot. A slit in the side of the form will keep the bottom thread out of the way while it is being wrapped. Fold the top thread out of the way.

3. Or, anchor fibers together after winding by using a needle to reach under the wound strands and securing with a stitch.

4. Slip a thin wire under the top loops of the tassel fibers when you wind them. Spread out the loops and wire them to the mold. For extra security, twist the wire every few wraps.

Created by Patricia Fox

*Gilded and beaded molds top these tassels by Patricia Fox.*

97

## USING BULLION FRINGE

Bullion fringe is a traditional skirt for both formal and folk tassels. While the word bullion means real gold or silver ingots, it has come to include twisted fiber elements, such as in bullion stitch. Bullion embroidery originally referred only to metal thread work. The term as used in tassel making probably derived from military fringe which is made from twisted gold metal. Whatever the material, bullion fringe is an important element in many tassels. It is made of short twisted ropes that are not cut. They are laid over a mold to create the illusion of fullness.

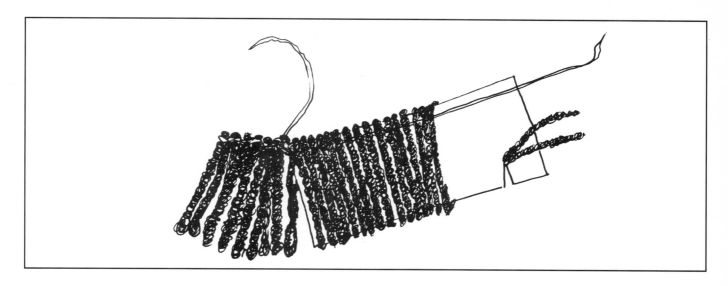

Referring to the diagram above:

1. Tightly twist a very long cord, but don't double it back on itself.

2. Wrap it an even number of times over a very sturdy cardboard form. Wire or stitch the top loops together in pairs while they are still on the form.

3. Slip off one pair at a time and twist them together in the opposite direction to form a rope. Continue twisting each pair to make a row of bullion fringe.

4. Wire or tie the fringe to the base of your mold.

*A collection of metal thread and bullion fringe tassels from Asia.*

## HIDING THE MECHANICS

The bottom edges of the mold covering, especially where the skirt is attached, don't have to pass rigid inspection because additional ropes, braids, or *ruche* can be added to form a border. Most commercial, and very expensive, tassels are made this way.

### *Try This!*

■ All sorts of overskirts can be added to the basic skirt. Commercial fringe, covered molds, individual pieces of bullion fringe, chains of flowers, pompons, strings of beads, or hand-tied macramé are just a few suggestions for dressing up the skirt of any tassel.

■ Sometimes a tassel needs to gain a little weight. Add extra yarns to any undernourished tassel by wiring or stitching on another skirt. Or, add yarns the way cords are attached (the tassel is treated as if it were the cord). The original skirt then becomes the "petticoat."

## FINISHING THE MOLDED TASSEL

Glue, stitch, or wire the ruche or other covering over the join between the skirt and the mold. String the covered mold onto the hanging cord. Secure the bottom of the cord with a large knot, a flange, or a bead large enough not to slip through the hole in the bottom of the mold. Attach the skirt either before or after securing the holding cord.

Referring to the diagram above:

1. To make a decorative ruche or "ruff", wrap matching threads around a rod to form tiny loops.

2. Secure with fine wire, remove from rod, and apply over the join.

3. An alternative is to make a ruche by wrapping yarn thickly around a narrow "U" shaped device, such as a lace crochet fork, until it is long enough to go around the skirt join. Stitch down the center by hand or on the sewing machine. Slip the ruche off the open end. Glue or wire to cover the join. Leave the loops or clip them to make a fuzzier band.

4. To make a ruche and skirt all in one, adjust the length of the "U" shaped device, as used in the "Embellishing with Flowers" section on page 78, to length plus ³/₄" of desired tassel. Wrap yarns close together for an area wide enough to fit around the circumference of the mold. Stitch very close to the top bar of the "U." Remove the yarns and secure to the mold. The narrow border at the top creates the ruche and the longer strands form the skirt. Leave the loops around the join or shear for a fur effect.

Fur collars were used on these tassels to conceal the joins.

### Try This!

- Round, flat shapes (buttons, rings, or shapes cut from cardboard) placed at the bottom of the mold make the skirt appear fuller and provide a place to anchor the cord. Metal washers double as flanges and add a nice weight.

- Add fancier yarns or a bullion fringe to this outside layer to save on materials. It is also an easy way to add stripes.

- Devise other techniques, such as using a row of smaller tassels, rick-rack, embroidered trims, or a covered ring to conceal as needed. Another quick fix is to chain gimp or soutache braids to form a ruche. A twisted band of fuzzy yarn, like chenille, is also an easy answer.

*A row of commercial bullion fringe was added over these original skirts. Jasmines, cords, and braids further decorate these tassels.*

Created by Lynn Sova

*This beaded-tassel headdress by Candace Kling is named "Red Rainbow."*

# TASSEL
## BEADING

### BEADED TASSELS

Beads and tassels seem to have an affinity for each other. The beads may decorate the tassel, the tassel enhance the beads, or the entire tassel be fabricated of beads. Beads offer the most glamorous way to add dazzle to your tassels.

**The earliest tassels were made from seeds, berries, shells, and bones; all of which are still used as tassel decorations today. Each culture has created unique designs.**

Beads were around thousands of years before Christ. They served as currency in many cultures. The development of beads since the first carved animal tooth is phenomenal. A visit to a bead store or a glance at a bead catalog will provide hours of inspiration.

Created by Carol Perrenoud

*Made from Italian vintage size 20 and 22 seed beads, this tassel is only two inches in length. These seed beads are equivalent to 900 beads per square inch.*

## CHOOSING A BEADING THREAD

The thread you choose for beading should be strong and ideally it should almost fill the hole in the bead. Polyester or polycore is good for sewing beads down. Always try to match the color of the thread to the background on which it is to be sewn.

Beads that will dangle are better threaded on fiber that won't stretch over time, such as bonded nylon and specially made beading threads. Bonded nylon comes in a wide color range, although it is cheaper and easier just to stick with a neutral color. It comes in sizes from C (thin) to FFF (thick). FF fits a #11 seed bead. Some beading threads are flat, which makes it easier to thread into the needle eye.

Monofilament fishing line, invisible sewing thread, or dental floss can be used in a pinch. Monofilament (even the best quality) will dry out when subjected to sun, so your dazzling tassel hanging in the window could become a pile of beads on the floor. Dental floss works well, but it frays very easily.

Whenever possible, use the beading thread doubled. To secure a knot in any thread, and still keep it flexible, use nail polish. Expensive polish is thicker and works better. Monofilament burned with a match forms a stopper bead at the end.

Created by Virginia L. Blakelock

*This koi bag, measuring 3¹/₂" x 20", shows loomwork using 272 beads per square inch.*

## THREADING THE NEEDLE

The first challenge in beading is to get the thread through a needle eye small enough to pass through the tiny hole in a bead. No matter how much you wet or twist the thread end, the needle often refuses to accept it.

Small glass beads, sizes 11, 12, or smaller, require 12, 13, up to size 16 (the smallest) needles. Buy several sizes and extras — they break! Assortment packs contain sizes 10 to 13. Quilting and milliners needles are other options.

**1. The eyes of beading needles are long and narrow, so prepare the thread to fit through the hole. Run the thread through beeswax to make it stiff and to prevent tangling and twisting. Cut a clean end and flatten it to a knife edge between your index finger and thumb or your teeth.**

**2. Use the best possible light; a magnifying lamp is even better. Steady your arms on the table, press your palms together, line up the flat edge of the thread with the eye of the needle, push, and pray!**

**3. Instead of trying to put the thread through the eye of the needle, hold the thread flat against your thumb and place the needle onto the thread.**

Created by Helen Dietz

108

## *Try This!*

■ Use pre-threaded silk or nylon beading thread, available in an assortment of colors. Stretch the thread first by hanging it over night with a fishing weight on the end.

■ Often, just doubling the thread keeps it from going through the bead hole. Taper stiff thread, like waxed nylon or linen, by lightly scraping off about an inch with a craft knife or razor blade to form a needle. See diagram below.

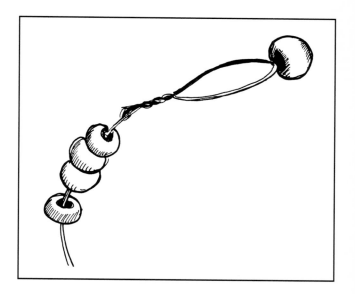

■ To prevent thread from fraying and tangling, run it over beeswax or soap. Twist the thread end to form a stiff point for inserting into the bead holes. Applying commercial fray preventative, glue, or nail polish to the flattened ends is also worth a try!

■ For large-holed beads, made a needle from thin brass wire. Clip off a few inches of wire and double it to form a large eye. Twist the cut ends together, leaving a loop. This is one needle you won't have trouble threading. Slip the beading thread in the loop and close the eye. See diagram at top right.

■ For large-holed beads, place the bead on a very fine crochet hook. Insert the hooked end into the fiber and the bead eased onto the thread. See diagram below.

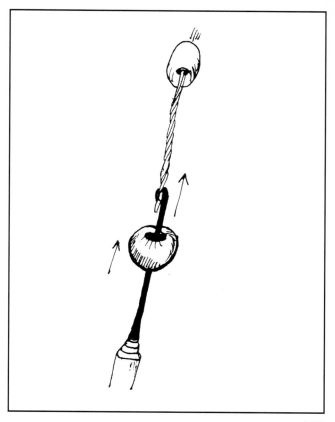

## SORTING BEADS

Keeping track of all those little beads while you're working can be a challenge. An artist's watercolor tray is useful to keep colors separated, but nothing will keep beads still for long — most seem to have a Mexican jumping bean ancestry! To accommodate this trait, release them on a velveteen cloth. They won't roll around and will submit to being speared with the needle. When finished working, wrap the tassel in the cloth with all the loose beads and tuck it away.

Keep beads in order to make stringing easier by placing them on a piece of double-sided tape that has been placed on your work surface.

*Sue Bonnin adorned antique hairpins with bead-trimmed tassels.*

Created by Barbara Leet

## MAKING BEADED TOPS

Barbara Leet shares her technique for creating beaded tassel tops.

1. To make this beaded top, start with 15 beads.

2. Divide the beads by color, designating each color by a letter. It may be easier to cover the head in one color for the first time so there is no pattern to follow.

3. String the beads, leaving about a 4" tail at the knotted end, as follows: 2 A beads, 1 B bead in this sequence until you have 15 all together. Bring the needle back through 6 beads to form a circle at the top of the head.

4. For the next row, string 1 A bead, 1 B bead, 1 A bead, bring the needle through the B bead in the circle above. Continue all the way around, finishing through a B bead. Come back through an A and B bead.

5. String 5 A beads, 1 B bead, 5 C beads in this sequence until the string is long enough to reach the tassel neck. Stitch through the neck wrap.

6. Return by stringing only A and C beads in groups of 5, connecting through the B bead.

7. At the crown of the tassel, come through the next B bead and string 2 A beads, come through the 3rd A bead, add 2 A beads, 1 B bead, 2 C beads, come through the 3rd C bead.

8. Continue this pattern to the neck of the tassel. Stitch to the neck wrap and return as before. Repeat to cover the entire head.

9. When you have made your last bite into the neck of the tassel, return as follows: 2 A beads, through the 3rd A bead, 2 A beads through B bead on the opposite side, to connect the pattern. Continue with 2 C beads, through the 3rd C bead, through the B beads on the opposite side. Continue to the crown. Come through the last B bead and thread through several beads before cutting the thread.

10. Wrap the tassel neck to cover the beading stitches.

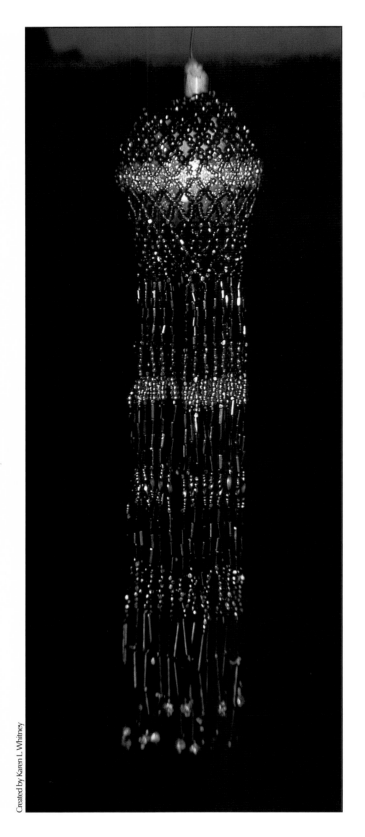

Referring to the diagram above:

1. To make a Peyote-stitch beaded top, form a circle of beads to fit the head or neck of your tassel.

2. Secure the ends tightly so the beads fit snugly.

3. On the same thread, string a bead and place it directly under the first (or last) bead in the ring.

4. Take the thread through the second bead in the ring, string another bead to lay under the third bead and secure through the fourth bead. Keep the thread tight as you work around to where you started.

NOTE: An odd number of beads makes it come out right, but, if you used an even number, drop down to start the next row and pass the thread through the last bead in the row above one more time. There will be three threads through that one bead. Designs can be created by changing the color of the beads.

## ADDING BEADS TO OTHER TOPS

If you don't have any particular tassel head in mind, use a small row of felt in the same or contrasting color as the beads. Couch strings of seed beads or pearls to this top, creating a solid head or a decorative pattern. See diagram below.

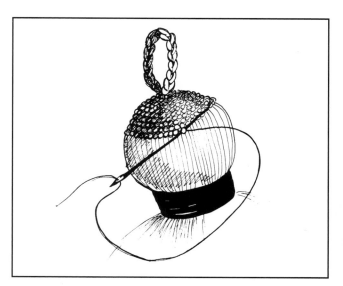

An intricately beaded tassel from India.

### Try This!

■ Intricately patterned heads for tassels can also be created on Indian wire beading looms.

■ String and stitch at the same time by stringing a few beads, then taking a backstitch into the tassel yarn. Bring the thread back through the last bead, string a few more, and secure it again with a backstitch. See diagram below.

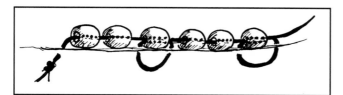

■ Prestrung beads instantly enhance the wrapping. Couch the strings by taking a small stitch over the beading thread between the beads and into the tassel yarns or mold covering. Tight curves, such as at the top, require frequent stitching. The couching thread can be invisible or decorative. See "Couching" on page 70. See diagram below.

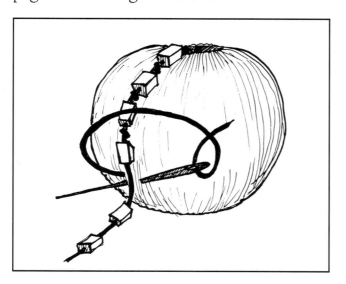

■ To solidly cover a mold that has a hole, bring the beaded string up the outside, pass the string alone up through the hole, then string more beads for each outside pass. See diagram below.

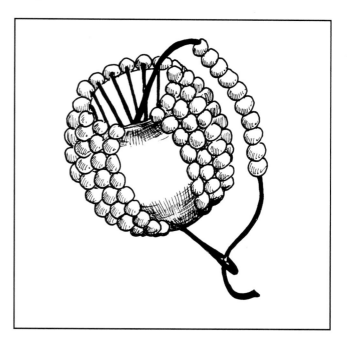

■ Use textured yarns to add beads. See diagram below.

■ Add French knots among the beads. See "French Knot" on page 72.

## MAKING BEADED SKIRTS

There are many ways to add a beaded skirt to a tassel top.

1. **To quickly add a beaded skirt to a tassel top, string your own assortment of beads or use purchased bead strings. Use the beads alone or add them over a yarn skirt.**

2. **To attach the bead strings to the tassel, use a needle and beading thread to pick up the thread the beads are strung on.**

3. **Stitch a loop of beading thread directly to the tassel head at regular intervals.**

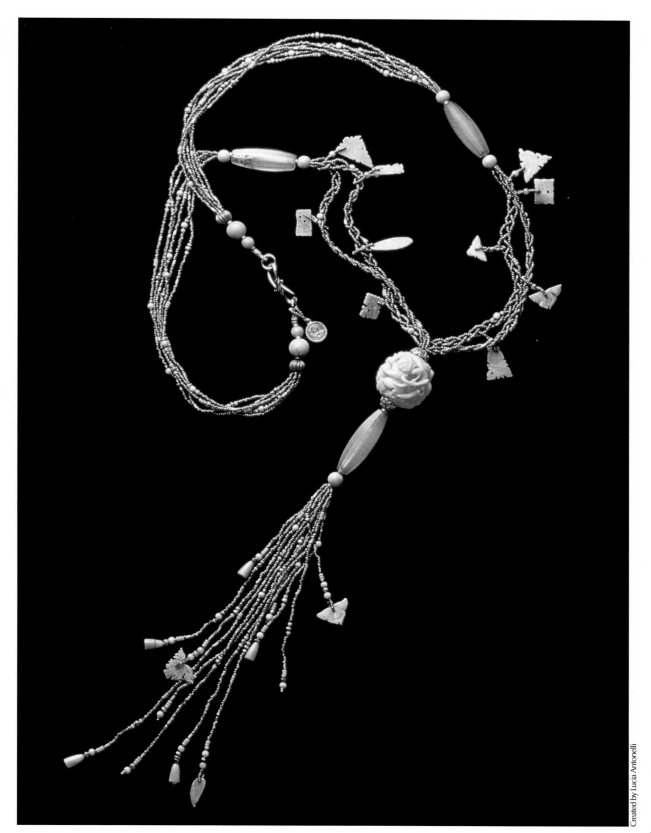

*Try This!*

■   For a fancier look, pick up a length of beads, then run the thread through a larger bead at the top. Bring the thread up through the bead before attaching it. Then return and pick up another length of beads, bring it up and attach. Use this technique to create a tassel on any soft surface.

■   Attach strings of beads to a separate tape, then roll to form a skirt.

To make single strands of fringe, string beads to the desired length, skip the end bead, and run the thread back up through all the beads. Then string another length and repeat. Stitch each strand to the tassel top as you go around. See diagram below.

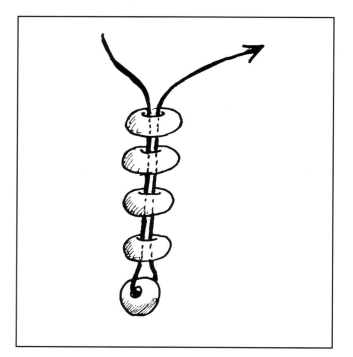

*Try This!*

■   Think ahead and couch a row of beads on the neck first, then thread the strand through one of the neck beads as you work around the tassel. Another row of horizontal beads can always be added at the neck to hide any glitches.

■   For a more decorative bottom finish, skip three beads before threading back up the strand to form a "flower" at the end. Or, add larger beads at the bottom to make a pronounced dangle. See diagram below.

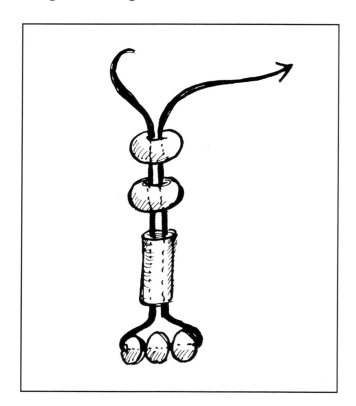

■ Vary the length of the strands and the color, size, and shape of the beads. Bugle beads give a different effect than seed beads, but combine nicely with them. See diagram below.

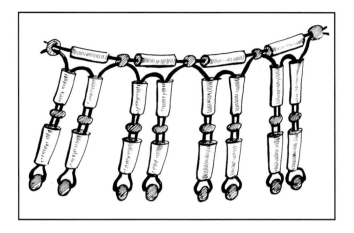

■ Similar to the technique for making looped fringe, cover the exposed wire with beads before bending. Make a loop in one end of a #20-gauge flexible wire and tie all the thread ends from the skirt onto the loop with overhand knots. Secure this knot with nail polish. When dry, cut off the thread ends and string beads on the remaining wire to cover the loop and make a hanger for the skirt. Bend the top of the wire with needlenose pliers to form a loop. The entire piece is stable and ready to be attached where you want it.

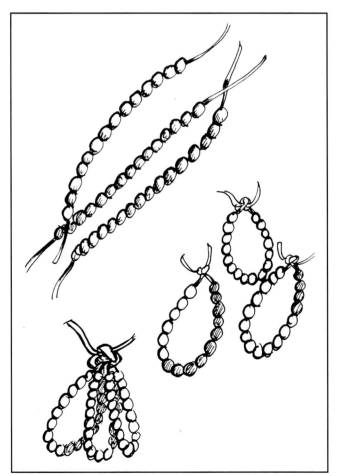

**Referring to the diagrams at left:**

**1. To add a beaded skirt to a tassel top with looped fringe, string groups of beads on separate threads, tie the ends together, leaving a little space between the knot and the beads so they will dangle nicely.**

**2. Secure the knot with a dab of glue or nail polish.**

**3. Thread a wire down through the tassel top and hook the clump of beads, then pull them into the top to hide the knots.**

**4. Bend the wire over at the top with needlenose pliers to form a loop and then stick the wire end into the top. A bead, large enough not to slip down into the hole, can be used to cover the wire loop.**

Becky Worsham stitches five small tassels, made in size 8 pearl cotton, together, over the cord, at the neck bindings. Then she stitches loops of beads over the tassel tops and up the cord. Some loops have a larger bead at the bottom, others are stitched in progressive lengths so they cascade down the tassel, while on others the loops form a curly top. This technique was taught by Susan Portra.

120

Referring to the diagrams at left:

1. To make open mesh bead work, begin as for the Peyote-stitch beaded top. Add several beads, then loop the thread back through this string and take a stitch through a bead in the row above.

2. Make another row of loops below the first. Weaving them together at the first junctions will make them less floppy.

3. Work with more than one thread (or wire for a stiff form) to create interlocking diamonds.

4. Larger beads can dangle from the last row. While you're at the bottom of the loop, add some extra dangles before you string the second half of the loop.

## MAKING MACHINE-STITCHED BEADED TASSELS

Yvonne Perez-Collins, a machine-embroidery teacher, shares her unusual technique for creating beaded tassels on the sewing machine.

The idea came to her while designing stamens for a lily. Her tassels have as many as 200 beads ranging from sequins to crystals.

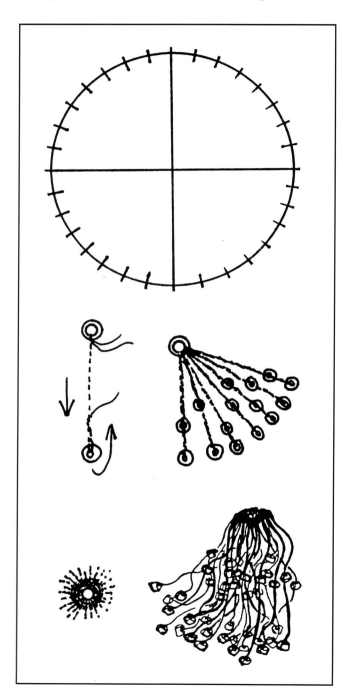

**Referring to the diagrams at left:**

**1. Draw lines on a layer of dissolvable fabric (Aquasolv®) and secure it in a 5″ spring hoop, then glue a jump ring in the center.**

**2. Set the sewing machine for zero length and width. Use machine-embroidery thread in top and bobbin. Remove the presser foot and lower or remove feed dogs. Use a size 60 or 70 needle, making certain all the beads can slide onto it. Lower the presser foot for sewing.**

**3. Take one stitch outside the jump ring and pull bobbin thread to the top. Turn the hand wheel and stitch inside the jump ring and then on the outside. Continue stitching toward the outer circle. To add a bead on the end, take one stitch into a bead and then stitch toward the center of the tassel. Add more beads along the way. The stitches should be on or over the first ones.**

**4. Repeat this procedure for every spoke or tassel strand. Finish by stitching around the outside of the jump rings three times. This will secure the threads. Trim the dissolvable fabric to within ¼″ of the stitching. Tie a string through the jump ring so the tassel can hang in a container of warm water for 20 minutes to remove the dissolvable fabric.**

Created by Yvonne Perez-Collins

123

## MAKING PAPER BEADS

For a circus of colorful beads, roll triangles of glossy wrapping paper or magazine pages croissant-style over a toothpick and glue. See diagrams below.

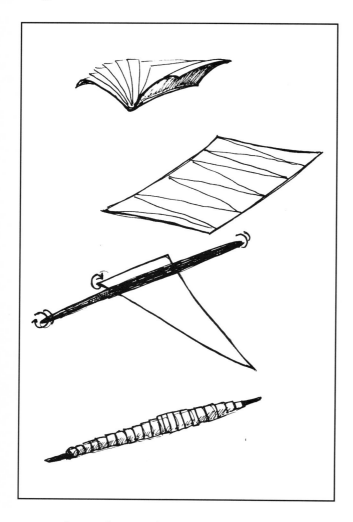

When glue is dry, coat the paper beads with a protective medium (wax, lacquer, clear acrylic, liquid plastic, etc.) and remove the toothpick. If desired, plastic straws can be used as forms and can be left inside the beads.

## *Try This!*

■   Vary the widths of the triangles to make long or fat beads.

■   Vary the shapes; rectangular strips make cylinders.

■   Use a craft knife and straightedge to cut the shapes.

■   Vary the paper; most kinds will work.

■   Design your own papers, using markers, rubber stamps, crayons, or watercolor.

■   Paint patterns on finished beads.

## DRILLING HOLES IN BEADS

Don't overlook coins, shells, and other materials. Even dried hunks of potatoes make interesting beads.

In primitive societies, holes are drilled in shells and coins by rolling a pointed stick between the hands rapidly while adding sand and water to act as an abrasive. You will find that a hand or electric drill work much easier!

Firmly tape the object to a board or push the object into floral clay held in a small container. Proceed to drill slowly and steadily. Water can be applied to the hole if the drill or object overheats. Always wear safety glasses and wear a mask to avoid inhaling drill dust.

*One of the most frustrating days of my life, my husband and I were leaving Madrid, Spain when we saw this enormous flea market. We had a few moments to spare and were wandering about when I spotted a booth of huge, ornate tassels. I could hardly contain myself until I realized we had almost no Spanish money left! I hauled out credit cards, traveler's checks, U. S. currency, even a personal check, but of course, all the seller wanted was money he recognized. By emptying both our wallets and with the help of a few tears, I was able to purchase the shabbiest of the lot.*

## AUTHOR'S REFLECTIONS

Tassel historian, Jim Rankin, sent me a copy of <u>ONCE A WEEK</u>, Vol. IV, published in London and dated December, 1860, to June, 1861. The following is quoted from a long article by Isabella Kentish entitled "TRIMMINGS AND TRIMMERS."

*"... Pausing a moment to cross the road, a group of grey-coated riflemen brush hastily past, and, as the simple braided uniforms meet our eye, we forget war and all its attendant miseries, and wander far away to the haunts of commerce, where that very trimming to the Volunteers' coats was manufactured. And this reminds us that the history of "Trimmings" still remains one of those things which ought to be and are not."*

She goes on to say that periodicals of the last fifty years have written: *"The Life, Death, and Last Ashes of a Cigar; The Tale of a Coat; History of a Pin; Adventures of a Needle; Walks of a Stocking; Glass-eyes, and those who use them; A Word on Wigs, by a hair-brained bald pate. But never, to our remembrance, do we recollect seeing one single word about 'Trimmings.' And without 'trimmings,' what would man or woman be? ... Kings and queens, warriors and statesmen, lawyers and clergymen, doctors and merchants, old ladies and young ladies, pretty women and ugly women, high and low, rich and poor, all pay their homage at the shrine of 'Trimmings;' and these few sheets shall be our offering to their departed glory."*

She then discusses the plight of the factory and piece worker, the low wages and demands of the job. *"... tassel molds are hanging like many-jointed, headless snakes upon the wall; while reels of silk and twist stand upon the counter, all ready to be given out with undisputed sway by a Mrs. Ellis through a sliding trap door, behind which the workers stand."*

Isabella Kentish concludes, *"And now farewell — a long farewell — to fancy trimmings."*

Dear Isabella,

I wish you had told us more about tassels and trimmers in the 1860s. Your few sheets have survived and so have tassels, but the history still remains "one of those things that ought to be and are not." We all still pay homage to trimmings, the working conditions have improved, but not many yet give credit to the painstaking handwork of the people who produce them. And we still have wars.

Here, then, are my few sheets to add a note from the waning days of the Twentieth Century. I hope they get dusted off in a few hundred years for some new tassel lover to discover, for I'm sure trimmings will still be around, it's only you and I that will have "departed."

And now ... farewell,
but not to fancy trimmings,

Nancy Welch, 1998

## THANKS

My grateful thanks to all the artists who contributed to this book. You provided outstanding inspiration for all tassel makers.

Loving hugs to my husband for his continuing help with photography, grammar, and the dishes.

To my daughter who always managed to squeeze one more tassel into her backpack.

Gail, I greatly appreciate your cheerfulness in the face of yet another tassel to draw.

Mary Black, my treasured award will never leave the mantle.

Sara Dower, Barbara Leet, Betsy Pinter, Tamara Carignan, Margo Carter Blair, Linda Colsh, Kate Richbourg, Carrie Arnold, Doris Waltho, "group," and other friends and tassel mates, my gratitude to you all.

## METRIC EQUIVALENCY CHART

| INCHES | MM | CM | INCHES | CM | INCHES | CM |
|---|---|---|---|---|---|---|
| $1/8$ | 3 | 0.9 | 9 | 22.9 | 30 | 76.2 |
| $1/4$ | 6 | 0.6 | 10 | 25.4 | 31 | 78.7 |
| $3/8$ | 10 | 1.0 | 11 | 27.9 | 32 | 81.3 |
| $1/2$ | 13 | 1.3 | 12 | 30.5 | 33 | 83.8 |
| $5/8$ | 16 | 1.6 | 13 | 33.0 | 34 | 86.4 |
| $3/4$ | 19 | 1.9 | 14 | 35.6 | 35 | 88.9 |
| $7/8$ | 22 | 2.2 | 15 | 38.1 | 36 | 91.4 |
| 1 | 25 | 2.5 | 16 | 40.6 | 37 | 94.0 |
| $1 1/4$ | 32 | 3.2 | 17 | 43.2 | 38 | 96.5 |
| $1 1/2$ | 38 | 3.8 | 18 | 45.7 | 39 | 99.1 |
| $1 3/4$ | 44 | 4.4 | 19 | 48.3 | 40 | 101.6 |
| 2 | 51 | 5.1 | 20 | 50.8 | 41 | 104.1 |
| $2 1/2$ | 64 | 6.4 | 21 | 53.3 | 42 | 106.7 |
| 3 | 76 | 7.6 | 22 | 55.9 | 43 | 109.2 |
| $3 1/2$ | 89 | 8.9 | 23 | 58.4 | 44 | 111.8 |
| 4 | 102 | 10.2 | 24 | 61.0 | 45 | 114.3 |
| $4 1/2$ | 114 | 11.4 | 25 | 63.5 | 46 | 116.8 |
| 5 | 127 | 12.7 | 26 | 66.0 | 47 | 119.4 |
| 6 | 152 | 15.2 | 27 | 68.6 | 48 | 121.9 |
| 7 | 178 | 17.8 | 28 | 71.1 | 49 | 124.5 |
| 8 | 203 | 20.3 | 29 | 73.7 | 50 | 127.0 |

| YARDS | METRES | YARDS | METRES | YARDS | METRES | YARDS | METRES | YARDS | METRES |
|---|---|---|---|---|---|---|---|---|---|
| $1/8$ | 0.11 | $2 1/8$ | 1.94 | $4 1/8$ | 3.77 | $6 1/8$ | 5.60 | $8 1/8$ | 7.43 |
| $1/4$ | 0.23 | $2 1/4$ | 2.06 | $4 1/4$ | 3.89 | $6 1/4$ | 5.72 | $8 1/4$ | 7.54 |
| $3/8$ | 0.34 | $2 3/8$ | 2.17 | $4 3/8$ | 4.00 | $6 3/8$ | 5.83 | $8 3/8$ | 7.66 |
| $1/2$ | 0.46 | $2 1/2$ | 2.29 | $4 1/2$ | 4.11 | $6 1/2$ | 5.94 | $8 1/2$ | 7.77 |
| $5/8$ | 0.57 | $2 5/8$ | 2.40 | $4 5/8$ | 4.23 | $6 5/8$ | 6.06 | $8 5/8$ | 7.89 |
| $3/4$ | 0.69 | $2 3/4$ | 2.51 | $4 3/4$ | 4.34 | $6 3/4$ | 6.17 | $8 3/4$ | 8.00 |
| $7/8$ | 0.80 | $2 7/8$ | 2.63 | $4 7/8$ | 4.46 | $6 7/8$ | 6.29 | $8 7/8$ | 8.12 |
| 1 | 0.91 | 3 | 2.74 | 5 | 4.57 | 7 | 6.40 | 9 | 8.23 |
| $1 1/8$ | 1.03 | $3 1/8$ | 2.86 | $5 1/8$ | 4.69 | $7 1/8$ | 6.52 | $9 1/8$ | 8.34 |
| $1 1/4$ | 1.14 | $3 1/4$ | 2.97 | $5 1/4$ | 4.80 | $7 1/4$ | 6.63 | $9 1/4$ | 8.46 |
| $1 3/8$ | 1.26 | $3 3/8$ | 3.09 | $5 3/8$ | 4.91 | $7 3/8$ | 6.74 | $9 3/8$ | 8.57 |
| $1 1/2$ | 1.37 | $3 1/2$ | 3.20 | $5 1/2$ | 5.03 | $7 1/2$ | 6.86 | $9 1/2$ | 8.69 |
| $1 5/8$ | 1.49 | $3 5/8$ | 3.31 | $5 5/8$ | 5.14 | $7 5/8$ | 6.97 | $9 5/8$ | 8.80 |
| $1 3/4$ | 1.60 | $3 3/4$ | 3.43 | $5 3/4$ | 5.26 | $7 3/4$ | 7.09 | $9 3/4$ | 8.92 |
| $1 7/8$ | 1.71 | $3 7/8$ | 3.54 | $5 7/8$ | 5.37 | $7 7/8$ | 7.20 | $9 7/8$ | 9.03 |
| 2 | 1.83 | 4 | 3.66 | 6 | 5.49 | 8 | 7.32 | 10 | 9.14 |

# Index